Family Trouble

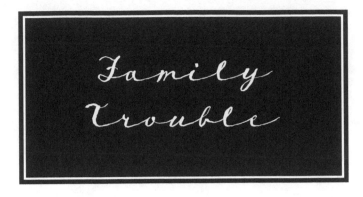

Memoirists on the
Hazards and Rewards of
Revealing Family

Edited and with an introduction by
JOY CASTRO

University of Nebraska Press
Lincoln and London

Library of Congress
Cataloging-in-Publication Data

Family trouble: memoirists
on the hazards and rewards of
revealing family / edited and with
an introduction by Joy Castro.
pages   cm
ISBN 978-0-8032-4692-8 (pbk.:
alk. paper) 1. Autobiography—
Authorship—Anecdotes.
2. Biographers—United States
—Anecdotes. 3. Family secrets—
Anecdotes. I. Castro, Joy, editor
of compilation.
CT25.F36 2013   808.06'692—dc23
2012048021

Set in Monotype Dante
by Laura Wellington.
Designed by A. Shahan.

Contents

Introduction

Mapping Hope

JOY CASTRO

Writers of all genres wrestle with the challenges, obligations, and consequences of including autobiographical material in their work. Which material is legitimately theirs to include, and whose stories should be discreetly omitted? How do their friends and families react when the work appears in print, on stage, or on screen? William Faulkner famously expressed his own notion of the artist's obligation to others in a 1956 interview in *Paris Review*: "The writer's only responsibility is to his art. He will be completely ruthless if he is a good one. . . . If a writer has to rob his mother, he will not hesitate; the 'Ode on a Grecian Urn' is worth any number of old ladies." When writing about family, where do writers draw the line? Do they rob their mothers, partners, children? Is *rob* the correct word for what they do?

For writers who publish memoir, these dilemmas are particularly acute, and memoir is the genre of our era. As James Atlas announced in the *New York Times Magazine* in 1996, "The Age of the Literary Memoir Is Now." Whole conferences and journals now focus on life-writing, scholarly books explore the memoir boom, and in creative writing programs everywhere, students eagerly practice the form. The world's largest scholarly organization devoted to the study of literature, the Modern Language Association, signaled its recognition of life-writing by dedicating its 2011 convention to the theme "Narrating Lives."

As the self-disclosing genre of our reality-hungry era, memoir offers few layers between the writer's private life and the words on the page. In her essay "The Bad Asian Daughter," Bich Minh Nguyen acknowledges the fact that "nonfiction has no cloak of make-believe to hide behind, no semantic scrim between narrator and author, speaker and author." By contrast, other genres provide their authors more cover: false names, new settings, a different ending to the story. "In fiction," observes Ariel Gore in her essay "The Part I Can't Tell You," "there are certain prices we do not have to pay." Memoir offers little such latitude.

When publishing memoir, writers pay the price of transparency, and the cost can become particularly dear when they write about family. With family stories, the stakes are always high, and there are choices both ethical and practical to be made at every stage. During drafting, writers make multiple determinations about which material is theirs to explore and which should be respectfully left out. Whose stories, intersecting with their own, constitute legitimate territory, and whose would be gratuitous to make public? If writers choose to include family material, do they retain their relatives' actual names, occupations, and other identifying information for the sake of transparency, or omit or alter such markers to protect privacy? How and when do writers inform their families that they're working on memoir projects? During revision, memoirists have the option of inviting feedback from family members. If they decide to invite input, how do they respect others' views yet set boundaries that preserve the integrity of their own vision? After publication, how do writers handle their families' reactions?

The *New York Times* devoted the piece "A Mother's Memoir, A Son's Anguish" to precisely this problem. "Are there limits to writing about loved ones, particularly one's children?" asks Julie Myerson, author of a controversial memoir about her son's drug addiction. David Sheff, whose memoir *Beautiful Boy* also explores a child's drug addiction, feels that "the imperative to protect a loved one, particularly a child, outweighs the responsibility to tell the truth"; Susan Cheever, memoirist and daughter of the autobiographical novelist John Cheever, disagrees. "I strongly believe everybody has the right to their own story," Cheever says, defining one's material as inclusive of the intersecting stories of family members: Cheever tried to bribe her five-year-old and twelve-year-old to get their approval to write about them. Weighing loved ones' privacy against the impulse to tell the desired story, writers draw different, difficult lines.

The writers included here in *Family Trouble* speak from a diverse range of perspectives as they explore ethical dilemmas, explain their practical strategies for each step of the writing and publishing process, and examine the barriers—internal and external—against writing about family. All of them have published work about family members; all have dealt with the consequences. They offer readers the sweet and bitter fruits of their experience.

The essays gathered here address memoirs about a marvelously wide range of family concerns, many of which have been viewed during past eras as illicit secrets. Adoption, for example, as both the rupture of family and the attempt to form family anew, is a key issue in essays by Susan Olding, Ralph Savarese, Susan Ito, and Karen Salyer McElmurray. Sexuality—particularly sexuality that refuses to fit neatly into the container of heterosexual marriage—forms another focus, as in Aaron Raz Link's "Things We Don't Talk About," about the process of writing *What Becomes You* (2008), the memoir of his sex change. Essays by Ariel Gore, Alison Bechdel, Judith Ortiz Cofer, and Sandra Scofield search for answers and narrative strategies in the wake of a family member's death, while Paul Austin and Ralph Savarese investigate the limits of parental responsibility in writing about children with disabilities. Other essays explore mental illness, abuse, neglect, and parental failures to provide and protect. Tackling these complicated and delicate issues, the writers articulate strong views on all sides.

Ethical consensus does not emerge. Some essays provide useful principles about where to draw lines, while others share painful cautionary tales. The pieces are funny, blistering, rugged, smart, generous, and warm by turns. All focus on the vexed dilemmas of including family members' stories in memoir—or, as Jill Christman puts it, "How will I know what is too private? How will I know when enough is enough?"

At the beginning of the twenty-first century, it seems, Faulkner's dictum does not hold. While Jill Christman and Alison Bechdel employ Faulkner's line about "any number of old ladies" as a touchstone, the writers in this collection share little of Faulkner's studied ruthlessness. Rather, their essays explore a clear recognition of responsibility toward loved ones—even a sense of moral anguish. In "Sally Could Delete Whatever She Wanted," emergency-room physician Paul Austin envisions his grown children decades from now, visiting him in retirement, where a copy of his ER memoir *Something for the Pain* (2008) sits on his bookshelf. "If they notice the book at all," he reflects, "I hope they will forgive the flaws in the way I've told our story. But in a deeper, more vital way, I hope they'll forgive my failings as a father." Stephanie Elizondo Griest "would rather pirouette off a bridge than hurt [her] parents in any way," as she confides in "The Seed Book." The memoirists in *Family Trouble* take their ethical responsibilities seriously. In "Like Rain on Dust," Richard Hoffman explains the challenge: "A memoir is not what happened, it is a re-presentation of what happened. The hyphen I've placed in that word represents all the literary skill and all the honesty and judgment that goes into writing a truthful book." These essays demonstrate that we can create honest, probing literary memoir while treating family concerns with care. "I am responsible," writes Jill Christman, "to more than art."

Indeed, rather than being careless about the bonds and obligations of family, these writers share an acute sensitivity to what family *should* and *can* be. When that vision of love and nurture goes awry, they feel compelled to write it, to right it. What family could have, should have been haunts them. As memoirists of family, these writers are pulled taut between the impulse to critique and the equally powerful impulse to empathize, understand, and forgive.

Family Trouble focuses on ethical choices and craft decisions, not legal concerns, since laws vary from place to place, change over time, and are subject to interpretation. These generous essayists, rather, share both their ethical deliberations and the practical strategies they employed at each step of the writing process, from drafting to post-publication. Neither prescriptive nor directive, the essays draw different boundaries and come to different conclusions. While Ralph Savarese's piece "I Might Be Famous" painstakingly unravels the many decisions he made as he shared his family's story with the world—on CNN, *Newsweek*, NPR, and ABC's *Nightly News*—he ends by saying candidly that he has "come to no definitive conclusions about what I did or what other writers should do." These writers simply dare "to enter," in the words of Aaron Raz Link, "the zones of tension that surround family stories," and to share what they've learned.

The essays also offer a series of clear, practical strategies for writers. Paul Austin asked not only his wife but also a family therapist to read his ER memoir "as an advocate" for his three children, while Ralph Savarese gave his son "the power to veto" the publication of *Reasonable People: A Memoir of Autism and Adoption* (2007). Bich Minh Nguyen let her sister read *Stealing Buddha's Dinner* (2007) in manuscript form; Allison Hedge Coke shared chapter drafts with her parents, sister, and son and invited their input; and Robin Hemley read his memoir aloud to his writer-mother, who suffered from glaucoma and macular degeneration. Aaron Raz Link shared his coauthored manuscript with family members before publication, explaining, "It seemed fair to give them the chance to offer their responses while our options for revision were still open." He and Ralph Savarese discuss their memoirs' innovations with sharing narrative control at the level of point of view: *What Becomes You*, Raz Link's memoir of his sex change, was coauthored with his mother, poet Hilda Raz, and Savarese's memoir *Reasonable People: A Memoir of Autism and Adoption* includes a final chapter that was written by his autistic son.

Many of the writers included in *Family Trouble* teach creative writing at universities and colleges and participate in the various professional activities of writers, and they offer here the fruits of those experiences. Several, including Robin Hemley, Dinty W. Moore, Mimi Schwartz, Sandra Scofield, Heather Sellers, and Sue William Silverman, have published noted creative writing texts for use in the college classroom. Jill Christman shares with readers the same suggestions she gives to her writing students, Ariel Gore explores the connection she feels to her students' eagerness and uncertainty, and Bich Minh Nguyen reflects upon her experience as a teacher of memoir. The writers in *Family Trouble* also share the common rhetorical situation of giving public readings. In "Mama's Voices," Susan Olding worries over reading an essay about her daughter publicly, concerned that it's "too revealing, too raw." Ruth Behar pulls no punches about the pain of family estrangement caused by her work in "The Day I Cried at Starbucks," and Lorraine López explores in "Calling Back" the celebration and fallout that occurred when her large extended family in New Mexico unexpectedly obtained copies of her first book and attended her reading en masse.

Numerous prohibitions and inhibitions discourage people from writing about their families, and the writers in this collection address those varied barriers. "We write, of course, against the tide of silence," explains Bich Minh Nguyen, "the same one that pushes people to say: *I'm not going to write about this until everyone else is gone.*" Often, the prohibitions come from within our own ranks, from other writers, from writing teachers and fellow learners. Workshopping material about her difficult, violent daughter at a writers' conference, Susan Olding faced classmates' explicit judgments: *"You'll ruin your daughter's life. . . . It's wrong to write about a child. . . . If you must write this, put it in a drawer."* Aaron Raz Link, too, was affected by advice received at writers' conferences. At one, he "listened to a teacher define bad nonfiction as 'stories about blood relatives and body parts'"— the very focus of his book—and at another, he "heard wise and well-known writers speak of the need to respect silence, to acknowledge the importance of both social boundaries and personal shame."

Social boundaries and personal shame can be intensified by specific ethnic and cultural prohibitions against putting family business out in the street. Bich Minh Nguyen calls memoir "an American form, not an Asian one" and explores the additional burden carried by writers of "ethnic" memoir, whose life stories are always read by the dominant culture as representing not just the family but the whole subculture. In "Memory Lessons," Rigoberto González describes facing the barrier of having "few models within the Latino literary landscape to learn from," and explores what he sees as the Latino/a writer's "inability to truly and without censorship air out the dirtiest items in the laundry basket. It's a cultural expectation: keep it within the walls of the home, honor the privacy of the living, respect the secrets of the dead." Such cultural prohibitions can have a silencing impact, and these essays discuss the courage needed to write one's way into essential family material. They offer encouragement, inspiration, and the reasons to persist.

For all writers of memoir, motivation is key. Ethical memoirists write in order to see, to understand, to come to terms with wounds. In "The True Story," Karen Salyer McElmurray concludes: "I can only say this: I wrote my life, page after page. Most importantly of all, I wrote about my family with the possibility of forgiveness."

In writing my own memoir, *The Truth Book* (2005), I knew far more about my family's private lives than I included. Two fundamental questions drove the writing of the book, urgent questions that baffled and hurt me: Why had my father killed himself? And why would a perfect stranger say that I had no personality? My hunch was that the two problems were inextricably linked, involving issues of self-erasure due to trauma. Yet when I began to draft, I couldn't be sure that my explorations of the past would end in illumination. "Good writing must do two things," contends Vivian Gornick in *The Situation and the Story: The Art of Personal Narrative* (2001). "It must be alive on the page, and it must persuade the reader that the writer is on a voyage of discovery." Writing *The Truth Book*, I truly was on a genuine voyage of discovery, and these two driving questions helped shape the memoir, guiding my choices about what to disclose and what to omit. If an incident, detail, or family story contributed in some way to the answering of one or both of those questions, then it went onto the page. If it didn't, I didn't even draft it. Thus, I left out material about my stepmother's difficult childhood and early first marriage, since it shed no light on either question. Similarly, while my own early first marriage certainly included elements of high drama, writing about my ex-husband would have lent little insight to the book's fundamental search. My son Grey, who figures intermittently in the narrative, was included only when he played a role in some turning point in the action or pivotal realization; *The Truth Book* features no adorable anecdotes, though his childhood included many. Likewise, though my husband has said and done many interesting, memorable things during our years together, I confined my descriptions of him only to those moments that bore directly on my search for understanding.

While this is partly a matter of respect for loved ones' privacy, it also stems from self-interest. Having worked so hard to build a happy family, I wanted to keep it, and people generally don't enjoy living with someone who is taking notes, viewing them as fodder. In "Calling Back," Lorraine López recalls the moment when "my youngest cousin, Juanita, regarded me in silence for a long moment before asking, 'All along, were you thinking like *that*? Were you thinking like a writer?'"

The essays in *Family Trouble* provide valuable cautionary tales, wrestling with doubt and illuminating those moments when excluding family material may actually be the best choice. Jill Christman, whose stepmother's "history of mental illness was so complicated, and sad," shares her decision "to leave her out of the memoir entirely." Paul Austin confesses his concerns about his daughter, who has Down syndrome, acknowledging that "there are passages in the book that would hurt her, if she could read them. Should I have left those passages out?" Rigoberto González highlights the dangers of "overthinking . . . overanalyzing . . . overscrutinizing" family memories "beneath the microscope of curiosity," and Sandra Scofield, the author of one published memoir, describes a moment when, faced with a trove of new family materials, she decided not to write another one. In her essay "Done with Grief: The Memoirist's Illusion," she dispels the hope that writing memoir will always function as catharsis.

The essays deal frankly with the risks and potential losses inherent in publishing about family. It's true that not everyone responds well. Ariel Gore's mother "read each inky page as betrayal," and Susan Ito describes how her birthmother, angry about her writing, stopped communicating with her for six years. In "At Its Center," Paul Lisicky copes with his aunt's ongoing outrage at being cast as a minor character—of having her complicated, demanding life reduced to an anecdote, however affectionately drawn—in his own memoir of growing up. In "Writing the Black Family Home," Faith Adiele bluntly analyzes the dynamic: "If you can't agree on an account of what happened last Thanksgiving, how could you ever agree on a version of your entire childhood? There are precautions you can take, concessions you can make, but ultimately you've demonstrated a power your family doesn't have. Be prepared to lose them." Lorraine López writes of the time her cousin "called me in Nashville and hung up on me. Twice. 'How could you?' she kept saying. 'How could you?'"

My own family's reactions were as multiple and varied as their personalities, their actions, and their stakes in maintaining the silence that had obscured our shared past for so long. Our stepmother, whose portrait in the book is mixed, surprised me by responding positively. Having once trained as a painter, she valued art for its own sake, and after *The Truth Book*'s publication, she sent me a congratulatory letter, praising the fact that I had managed to make art out of all the chaos. She then slipped permanently from our lives. By contrast, the response of the adoptive mother who raised me—who features largely in the book and had already rejected me for not sharing her religious beliefs as a Jehovah's Witness—was more predictable. When notified about the book's impending publication, she sent only a brief email: "I can't deal with you right now." Several years later, she still hasn't. To my knowledge, she hasn't read the book—which is sad, because writing it helped me understand the difficult situation she'd faced and increased my compassion for her destructive choices. While publishing my story cost me that relationship definitively, it wasn't a relationship I'd really had in the first place. Her sister, though, has since read it and reached out to me, as have my other aunts and cousins. My birthmother surprised me by reacting not to the story of her attempt to abort me, but to the description of her hair. "It was a *perm*," she said, perturbed. Perhaps some things are too big, too painful, to discuss. My biological father, a lifelong alcohol abuser, reacted with drunken outrage at the minimal role he played in the text, though his actual part in my life had been no bigger.

The only member of my family of origin with whom I shared the manuscript before it went into production was my cherished younger brother, both because he was the only person from that time whose love I still enjoyed, and because the book represents him at his most painfully vulnerable—as a starved, abused, neglected child—and I felt he deserved to share control. As a girl, I had sometimes managed to protect him and sometimes failed. While I wanted to explore my own story, which was inextricably his story as well, I desperately wanted him not to be hurt again, didn't want my work to be a reinscription of old wounds, an unwanted exposure, an exploitation. In the original manuscript, I worked hard to protect his privacy, including leaving his name out of the narrative, referring to him throughout only as "my brother" and "my little brother." I sent him the electronic file with the carte-blanche promise to make any changes he requested.

I dug in to wait, expecting his reading of the manuscript to take a while, since he usually took time to respond, if he responded at all, to anything emotional or relating to our childhood. I was very nervous.

But he printed the manuscript immediately and spent a weekend passing pages back and forth with his girlfriend. When he called back, he wasn't ashamed, wasn't afraid of the exposure. He was proud of what we'd survived, and he felt it was an important story to tell. "You put my name in there," he said.

While the publication of a family memoir can offer relatives a chance to move, grow, and communicate in new ways, what I've experienced is that people will largely continue to be themselves, just more intensely. Warm alliances will be strengthened; angry people will lash out; relationships that weren't really functional will fall quietly away.

How family members react is not in your hands, I tell my memoir-writing students. What *is* in your hands is the narrative: its fidelity to facts as you recall them, its fair-mindedness, its compassion for the straits in which your family members found themselves, its sincere quest to understand what happened. "Intention matters," as Jill

Christman writes. Motivation matters, and it affects the integrity of the work you produce. "Do not do this work in order to be seen, to be right," counsels Heather Sellers. "Do it in order to see."

Write, I tell my students. You cannot predict what will offend someone, so just write. You can always revise, emend, edit. This lesson is borne out by the essays here: Bich Minh Nguyen calls for "a little ruthlessness" in the original drafting process: "write everything down first; pare away later." With publication, people may get angry about things written with no intended malice, because their portraits on the page don't jibe with the images of themselves they cherish. As Paul Lisicky concludes: "The lesson is obvious but simple: we have absolutely no control over how others interpret our work, even when we think we're writing out of affection." Jill Christman concurs: "Here is the lesson: when you're sitting at your desk, recreating the lives of your loved ones on the page for all to see, you cannot anticipate what will rub someone wrong. You think you can, and this inner, anticipatory critic, will hang you up. She will hold you by the ear and squeeze. Shake her off. She doesn't know. The things she thinks will offend will not offend. The things she can't even imagine will offend . . . she will let slide unnoticed. Shake her off. Write your story."

Aaron Raz Link agrees, noting that "the closest I came to a permanent rift with my brother was over the appropriate word to use when describing his residence: 'townhouse' or 'townhome.'" Ruth Behar's experience with her uncle, who objected to specific words—"tiny," "rundown," "godfather"—was similar. Aaron Raz Link's conclusion about family sensitivities: "You just never know."

One reward of the difficult work of autobiographical writing is finding clarity and coming to understand the past. In "The Deeper End of the Quarry: Fiction, Nonfiction, and the Family Dilemma," Dinty W. Moore suggests the importance of such work. "What I believe," he writes, "is that the straightforward telling of family stories has value. I believe that more people have been harmed over time by secrets and concealment than by candor and revelation." In "Your Mother Should Know," Sue William Silverman, whose two memoirs cover both childhood sexual abuse and its long-term impact, concludes, "Now, after writing my secrets, the weight of life feels lighter. Without the burden of living a double, splintered life, I'm whole." Judith Ortiz Cofer feels that "only by writing" her deceased father's story "would I know how his life narrative has shaped mine." Karen Salyer McElmurray offers her realization: "As I wrote a memoir about family—about my own mother, myself as a mother, about the son I'd surrendered—my depression shifted, and so did the way my story was told. . . . In writing my memoir about family, I began to see how the pieces fit."

In dissolving secrecy and shame, memoirists reach past isolation and toward others. "Communication leads to community," as Jill Christman writes, "and community sustains us." Sometimes this happens quite literally, within writers' own families. Sue William Silverman's extended family, whom she had never known, reconnected with her after reading her first memoir, *Because I Remember Terror, Father, I Remember You* (1996). After the publication of his memoir *Half the House* (1995), Richard Hoffman and his father enjoyed a new closeness, and the publication of *Stealing Buddha's Dinner* led Bich Minh Nguyen's formerly uncommunicative family to acknowledge "the idea that our experiences were worth writing about." She marvels, "My family talks so much when we're together now." For Mimi Schwartz, sharing with her husband the draft of her marriage memoir *Thoughts from a Queen-Sized Bed* (2002) "helped a drifting marriage onto more emotionally solid ground." In one of the most moving incidents in this collection, Lorraine López describes the moment she saw her cousin Molly, from whom she'd been estranged due to the portrait of her in López's first book: "Without thinking, I rose from my seat and crossed the room to embrace her. She hugged me back. 'I can't be mad at you anymore,' she said. 'I was angry for a long time, and then I started writing.' Molly pulled a sheaf of papers from her oversized handbag. 'I always wanted to write, and you made me want to write my side.'"

While family bonds can be strengthened by the publication of memoir, sometimes the building of community occurs on a larger, public scale. Paul Austin hopes that through his disclosure of his own ambivalent feelings about work and fatherhood, some father may gain comfort, knowing he wasn't the only one. Ariel Gore explains her motivation for disclosing her life and her family in memoir: "I write it because I want to tell you that if your life and your grief feel messy and shameful sometimes, too, that maybe it's not just you—you're like me, and we're everybody."

When I was thirteen in West Virginia, abused and underfed, living in a trailer twelve miles from the nearest town, I didn't know why I drew floor plans of houses—in scraps of free time, on scraps of paper: houses with swimming pools and palm trees, houses with attached stables for my imagined horses, houses where an older boy would visit and fall in love with me. I drew houses of safety, sufficiency, of plenitude and pleasure. I hid them.

When I first read the essays collected here, I learned that Heather Sellers—who grew up through her parents' mental illness and alcohol abuse—also drew house plans as a child. In an early version of her essay, she explains, "I wasn't going to become an architect, ever. I was becoming a self, drafting and organizing a personality. I was mapping a blueprint for hope."

Geographical and architectural metaphors infuse several of these essays, which reflect on the way that memoirs remap domestic space and reconfigure what the structures of *home* and *family* can mean. As Aaron Raz Link points out, "Like architects, writers mark borders separating personal spaces from public ones." Writing about her silenced status as her birthmother's guilty secret, Susan Ito metaphorizes adoption as "Living in Someone Else's Closet."

Memoir politicizes the personal, and the essays in this collection recognize the political work that family narratives accomplish in the wider world. To which nation do we belong? Which family? On which side of the border do we stand? Susan Ito traces her Japanese American birthmother's need for silence and secrecy back to a life shaped by prejudice and World War II–era internment camps. Of her Nigerian Finnish Swedish heritage, Faith Adiele observes, "I am heir to family-group histories that have been at best underrepresented, at worst misrepresented. My job is to wield memoir as the corrective."

While the immediate concerns of memoirists may seem tightly focused, the ultimate ramifications of our work expand well beyond the private sphere. As Bich Minh Nguyen explains, "To tell the stories of family is to break the divide between inside and outside."

Memoir argues, directly or implicitly, for how the family should be configured: how parents should act, how children should be treated, and how the broader culture should dignify or ignore the rights of its varied and vulnerable citizens—the autistic, the abandoned, the abused, the queer, the dark, the poor. Aaron Raz Link writes: "Before I became a writer, I was a historian working in public museums. As a result, I see that [the concept of] *family* assembles our individual stories together to form larger stories, which are assembled together to become the fabric we call *culture* and *history*. This process gives each of us some sense of belonging to a larger world. The stories themselves provide the explanations we are given for the shapes and meanings of our lives."

"Memoir . . . is seen as a kind of record," writes Bich Minh Nguyen. "And to enter into this record-keeping is to assert, audaciously, a point of view." To reconfigure the family—our most basic, intimate unit of community—is to rebuild the world.

Audacious, yes. Yet also open, curious, willing to invite and hear other versions. In writing about family, memoirists draw others—their family members, the wider world—into the conversation about how to structure relationships. Ralph Savarese, considering issues of perspective, writes, "I delighted in my son's disagreement; another view had collided with my own, thereby complicating each. We'd usefully staged the problem of point-of-view, as fundamental as it is inescapable." Rigoberto González acknowledges, "I know that what I write down is simply my version, not the definitive, unchallengeable truth." Audacious yet humble, assertive yet listening: family memoirists negotiate the tensions of speaking the self while dwelling in relationship. "What we can tell is ours to tell," writes Aaron Raz Link. "Everything we can't tell is someone else's story—someone who may or may not speak, and who may or may not agree with us. We can only leave space in our lives and work for these voices to be heard."

I
Drawing Lines

Chewing Band-Aids

One Memoirist's Take on the Telling of Family Secrets

JILL CHRISTMAN

Every time I give a public reading from my memoir *Darkroom: A Family Exposure*, someone wants to know: "In your book, you reveal a lot of really personal information. How did your family react?" Look at my subtitle. If anyone has brought this question upon herself, it's me. I accept that, but I'm guessing I'm not the only memoirist to field this question on a regular basis. In fact, if I were a betting woman, I'd venture to say that after at least 90 percent of memoir readings, some variant of this question gets called out into the room.

I am not criticizing a lack of imagination in the good, good people who attend literary readings.

(And in fact, in a post-Frey world, I much prefer it to its sister question, which is essentially: "Are all memoirists dirty, rotten, self-serving liars?" Ummm. No.)

But the family-reaction question is complex. Let's think for a moment about what this question might mean.

Perhaps the asker wants to know how we memoirists get away with being so cavalier with our family's privacy. How do you live with yourself? How do you sleep at night when you've betrayed your family's deepest and darkest?

Is the question, then, an implicit condemnation of what we memoirists do?

Alternately, I wonder if the question is a kind of permission seeking. How'd it come out in the end? How'd you pull it off? Can I do this? Is it okay? Hey, Memoir Lady, can I tell my story too?

Or is the question asked with more salacious intent? Is it a barbed hook in the water to see what other fishy secrets can be pulled to the surface? What did you choose *not* to tell us that would have really pissed off your family? What are you still holding back?

Or maybe the asker is a writer himself, and slyly—we writers are nothing if not sly—wants to insinuate that the publication of your memoir has to do, not with the writing, but rather with your willingness to expose your family to public scrutiny. Had his life contained such drama, *and* had he been the sort of person who was willing to flap his family's laundry in the literary wind, well then, he'd be the one standing at the podium and taking questions about his personal life.

Or, I suppose, maybe the question is simpler than all that. Maybe the asker just wants to hear how your family reacted. Maybe she simply figures that this is the stuff of a good story.

I gauge my answer to my audience.

If the faces look friendly, I give a little background information. I confess my former naiveté. Before I started writing *Darkroom*, the only thing I'd ever published was a short story about a trucker in the booklet handed out to parents at the end of the summer arts program. I was clueless.

Nevertheless, nearing thirty and enrolled in a graduate writing program, I must have understood on some level that the reason I wrote was to some day get that writing published. But I'll tell you now—though at least half of you won't believe me—I didn't really understand what I was signing up for when I documented in my then-thesis, for example, the day I told my father that "he'd never been much of a father." That's on page 1. Or when, after describing my brother's near-fatal burning in the bathtub and my parents' subsequent separation, I revealed that the primary reason my mother reconciled with my father three years later was because she "wanted to have a baby that matched." (That's me—the amazing matching baby.) Or, a couple chapters later, when I told the whole story behind my uncle Mark's million-dollar marijuana growing operation in the cornfields of northeastern Washington. (Now we've arrived at a line I wouldn't have crossed under different circumstances. When I started writing *Darkroom*, my uncle was already in prison serving time for that marijuana. He'd been caught and convicted. If not, I certainly wouldn't have provided evidence against him. I was naïve, not stupid, and I wasn't raised a rat.)

So on some level, I got it: when writing gets published, if we're lucky, someone out there reads it—but I lacked a gut-deep awareness of what that kind of honest revelation would mean to my family, and to me. I had gotten caught up in the telling of my story. I never sat at the keyboard conjuring images of different people reading a book, my book, and gasping with each successive revelation. No. I just wrote. I was alone in a room with my computer and I felt perfectly secluded and safe.

Then the book was accepted for publication, and I was hit with a jolt of panic and burgeoning sense. Those of you who have been eight months pregnant might know this sensation. Do you know that feeling of looking down at your bulging, tight belly and realizing—for the first time, really understanding—what's going to happen next? Shit! Oh! Shitshitshitshit. This baby has got to *come out*. One way or another, this baby is *coming out*. That's what word of *Darkroom*'s impending publication felt like to me. Just like an unborn baby, it was exciting, so exciting, the only thing I could think about, and also: terrifying. I was repentant. For a full month, I stumbled around muttering: *What have I done?!?*

My family had cooperated in the writing of the book. They were all generous with their stories, but on the news of publication, they too gained a new understanding. My brother, Ian, had been bragging to his friends and colleagues, "The good news is my sister wrote a book!" (I believe he was genuinely proud of this fact.) Then he would pull out the punch line. "The bad news is that it's about us." Ba-dum-bum chhh.

Before the book release date rolled around, Ian's joke was funny, but a week afterward, he and my sister-in-law called from their home in Georgia, a thousand miles away, each chiming in on a different extension. Turns out they'd ordered up two copies of *Darkroom* from Amazon so that they could read simultaneously and compare notes. They informed me of this situation, and we all let a buzzing silence linger on the line. The plastic spine of the handset slipped a bit in my damp palm and I felt my heart crawl up into my throat like a salamander into a pool drain. Slimy. Doomed.

"So," my brother said finally. "I've got a bone to pick with you." (This choice of phrasing was especially eerie because the only person I'd known to use this phrase regularly was my stepmother, whose history of mental illness was so complicated, and sad, that I had elected to leave her out of the memoir entirely. So there's another line I didn't cross. Also, since her life intersected only tangentially with mine, it wasn't *necessary* to my story to tell her story, so I did not.) In the seconds that followed my brother's opening, I considered possible points of contention, flipping pages in my mind, a kind of literary flashing of the life before the eyes: the personal details of his near-death burning, the responsibility he might feel for my six years of sexual abuse at the hands of our neighbor (his friend), the revelation of my grandfather's alcoholism, my uncle's alcoholism—shoot, a whole family leaning toward the self-medication of drugs and alcohol . . .

No. My brother continued. "In the scene in the restaurant where Dad gets the Band-Aid in his mouth . . ."

Yes? Yes? My heart was truly and sincerely battering against my ribs now like that same salamander, caught in the bucket of an eager six-year-old, frantically dog-paddling its flapping feet against the smooth wall. Flap flap flap. *I've got a bone to pick with you.*

"Well, you have Dad chewing on that Band-Aid like a bunch of times. He didn't chew on the Band-Aid that long. He chewed maybe twice before he spit it out. That's it."

That's it. Wait! That's *it*? A whole book brimming with abuse and death and drugs and betrayal and . . . and he's hung up on how many times Dad *chewed*?

My salamander heart slid out of the overturned bucket, found purchase in the grass, and scampered into the cool shade of a damp rock. What a relief.

Here is an excerpt from the scene in question—my mother, father, brother, and I are sharing a rare meal during what we called the "kid swap" at a restaurant halfway between my mother's house in Massachusetts and my father's house in Connecticut:

[M]y father was munching away happily on his nicely mounded slaw, which could have been fresh coconut ice cream, from the scooped, snowy looks of it, except for the occasional orange carrot fleck that was prodded out of the pile by my father's insistent fork.

I watched my father chew. His cheeks bulged with the bulk of a generous forkful of slaw, making the hairs of his thick, closely trimmed beard move like a hedgehog trying to get comfortable. I remember seeing a change come over his face as his munching ground to a slow stop. The corners of his mouth pulled down in an expression of early disgust, and his soft, pink, lower lip emerged from its covering of beard and mustache. He took one more test chew, grimaced, and stuck out his tongue. On the end of his tongue sat a folded Band-Aid.

"Oh, man, gross!" my brother yelled, lifting the bun from his burger and checking under the green disc of pickle for any foreign objects that might have been hidden in his slice of melted American cheese.

"Ewwwww," I squealed.

"Oh, yuck," my mother said.

My father made no sound. He removed the Band-Aid from his extended tongue, and using both hands, unfolded it. When he had the non-stick pad exposed, he lowered his chin towards his chest, entirely occluding his neck, and peered over the top of his wire-rimmed glasses at the offending Band-Aid. His lower lip re-emerged from its hairy recess and began to tremble. "There's a scab," he said. "There's a Band-Aid with a scab in my coleslaw."

My brother didn't object to the scene itself. He took no umbrage with my description of the coleslaw, the Band-Aid, or the nasty scab. Nope. He thought I was exaggerating the number of times my father's teeth closed. (James Frey, David Sedaris, and Peggy Seltzer would love to have my problems, eh?)

I had a point in including this scene in the book. The scene continues through the bill paying and settles on the fact that my father actually *paid* for the infected coleslaw, although we did all get free ice cream in compensation for my father's pain and suffering. I use this as evidence that my father might be spineless. Or maybe gentle. Or perhaps both.

But more than twenty years after that scabby Band-Aid hit my father's teeth, my assessment of my father's character is not my brother's concern. He wants me to know that there was not quite so much chewing. Okay. I concede the point that I can't remember precisely. I am shaking with relief when I hang up the phone.

Here is the lesson: when you're sitting at your desk, recreating the lives of your loved ones on the page for all to see, you cannot anticipate what will rub someone wrong. You think you can, and this inner, anticipatory critic will hang you up. She will hold you by the ear and squeeze. Shake her off. She doesn't know. The things she thinks will offend will not offend. The things she can't even imagine will offend, the things she lets you tap tap tap right over—the chew count, for heaven's sake—she will let slide unnoticed. Shake her off. Write your story.

Here is the secondary lesson for me. Intention matters. If you set out to bring down your family, they will know. (This is your prerogative, by the way. Maybe they deserve it. But I can pretty much bet there will be familial fallout.) If you set out to answer a question for yourself, something that's important to you, to them, to art—they will know that, too. I know that there were moments in my book that hurt people I love. My mother had to read about how I had suffered at the hands of our neighbor, which she had never known. She failed to protect me. I am a mother myself now, and I can't imagine the pain of being face-to-face with that kind of knowledge and responsibility. My mother is the only member of my family who read *Darkroom* while it was still in draft. She cried a lot at first, but in the end, she did not add to the existing pain. She stood back and let me tell my story.

So to answer the question: How did my family react? Well, pretty damn well, actually. My brother's criticism began and ended with the chewing. The third time my mother read *Darkroom*, she called to tell me she thought the book was "beautiful." She maintains that I misrepresent her advice regarding a mate—"My mother suggests that I choose a father who wouldn't fight for custody in a break-up"—but she made her retraction before the book was published, and I put her objection right there in the book. I *said* she says she did not say this thing she says she didn't say. We remember that conversation differently. This is not so uncommon in families. *Still*, she says. *That was tricky*. Maybe she's right. But my mother adores me. She would forgive me anything. My father? My relationship with him was nearly nonexistent before *Darkroom* was published, and now—well, now things are a bit better. The writing healed my own heart. I hold nothing against him. He was a lousy father to me, we both agree on that, but he's been better with his subsequent children, and I can admire a man for trying to improve, for learning. Occasionally, one of his graduate students will e-mail me with a question about some point in the book. They'll tell me he passed the book on to them to help with some aesthetic or personal struggle. Wow, I think. Amazing.

Maybe I just got lucky. Maybe because I hail from a family of artists—dysfunctional though we all might be—I can get away with more. My family believes in art. I make art. They understand that, and they let me do what I need to do.

So that's my story, and it has such a tidy resolution. Why, it's practically a happy ending! But the question—*How did your family react?*—won't hold still for me. Five years after the publication of *Darkroom*, it's dawning on me that this is what I do. I use my body and brain and gut as a filter to understand the world. I didn't write *Darkroom*, as I once assured my family (and believed myself) to get my childhood out of my system, out of the way, so I could return to fiction writing and leave them all in peace. No.

Turns out I'm a serial memoirist, so it's no small wonder that this question of family revelation has reached a new level. Faulkner may have been on to something when he said in that famous *Paris Review* interview that "the 'Ode on a Grecian Urn' is worth any number of old ladies," but it's one thing to rob your mother for good work— she's a grownup, after all. By the time you're old enough to take up the pen and do the deed, well, she's probably done something to deserve a little calling out. She can take it. But what if we tip this notion down to the next generation, the one still coming up?

Since *Darkroom*, I have had two children, one of whom is squirming in my lap, cooing, as I type this. I'm making an adequately amusing click-y sound, and the motion of my fingers almost looks like a tickle, but beyond those possibilities, Huck has no idea what I'm doing. He's only three months old. He didn't sign up for this, and lately I find myself longing a bit for the supposed anonymity of a different genre.

One afternoon my very private poet husband—poor man, what could he have been thinking, marrying me?—snapped under the gaze of my writer's eye. "You know what?" he growled. "I wish we had our whole life on videotape so I could rewind and show you that you're *wrong*. Why don't you write that down and put it in your next fucking book?" Naturally, I wrote it down.

But what about this moment? I'm in my bedroom with my baby, both of us in our pajamas, playing a bit between napping and nursing, and here I go writing it. It's hard to imagine that Huck would ever care to read these words (yawn), but if he did, what would he think? Would he feel his privacy betrayed? My love and memory for these intimate moments with him somehow changed? And if he's not concerned with this image of himself in the perfect innocence of his preverbal infancy, then later? I mean, what is there to say about Huck now? That his feet were so big at birth the nurse couldn't even get the print on the hospital sticker? That his wide, lopsided smile makes my heart beat like first love? There's not much to object to there. But what if when he's in middle school he uses one of those big feet to trip another kid, and we end up in the principal's office together to discuss the details of his detention? (Okay, okay, so shoot me for not wanting to imagine in print more serious transgressions that might land us in that room together.) And what if that conversation raises interesting issues about kindness, and I want to use that scene with my son as the foundation for an essay? I don't know the answer to that question yet, but it feels so much more complicated to me. I'm thinking I might need to move into another subject area as my children grow. But how will I know where that line is? How will I know what is too private? How will I know when enough is enough?

I began with the intention of answering, fully and honestly, a question I have been asked many times: *How did your family react?* I set out to tell a story and maybe proffer the nuggets of my experience, but instead I have written myself up against an unanswerable question. In the same interview in which Faulkner sacrificed all those old ladies to the work, he said, "A man's moral conscience is the curse he had to accept from the gods in order to gain from them the right to dream." Substitute "raise children" for "dream" and you'll see where I find myself as a writer—a memoirist—and a mother.

Important stories will grow out of my life with my kids, and I will want to write them down, think about them, dream, but I will be watching myself more closely. I am no longer protected by naiveté— at least not of the sort I can recognize from where I sit with this baby in my lap.

From here forward, I imagine myself failing to take the advice I offer to students in every memoir class I teach: *Don't worry about what your family will think. Not yet, anyway. What you imagine now will offend, injure, or disrupt is probably the wrong thing. You have no way of knowing, so give it up, and get down to business. Get writing. Tell your version of the story. It is yours. You own it. If you tell your own truth, you cannot go wrong.*

I believe I am telling my students the truth.

But where does my story give over to my children? When does our story together become theirs to tell? Or *not* to tell, as only they can choose? On this side of the birth order, the rules seem different to me. Now I have a new set of imagined critics—my own children, grown up and reading—watching me as I write.

Glancing over my shoulder, I whisper, *I'm sorry. I'll be careful, sweeties. I promise to be careful.*

I am responsible to more than art.

While I can't imagine a time when I would give my children—or anyone—veto power over my writing, I've begun this conversation about privacy and publication with my daughter and recognize that my children's capacity to articulate their own needs regarding public exposure will likely parallel the needs themselves. As my children grow, I will talk to them about my writing—and all things. Already, Ella has announced her intention to pursue three simultaneous vocations—teaching, inventing, and yes, writing.

No doubt she will have stories to tell about her mother.

Here's something I don't typically tell my students, perhaps because it has less to do with writing and more to do with how I want to live in this world: secrets help no one. Maybe it's because I'm a survivor of sexual abuse and I know the danger of a well-kept secret. The secrets of my childhood mutated, dividing and growing into malignant cells of shame and isolation, multiplying until I had the choice to cut them out or be consumed.

Writing *Darkroom* was healing for me, and to a lesser degree for my entire family. I'm finished with secrets, and I know my determination to live in the light of full exposure has led me not only to memoir, but to my children themselves. Art and life, life and art—so famously fraught.

My children will be raised in the belief that we're all better off if we live an open life. Communication leads to community, and community sustains us. I believe that as deeply as I believe anything. And then there's this other true thing: I value our lives with our children, and our children's lives, as *lives*. Intimacy and exposure can be incompatible, but privacy and secret keeping are not the same. The Latin root of "private" is simply "not in public life," but tracing "secret" to its conception takes us to a darker, lonelier place—*secretus*, to set aside or apart. I want to live with my family in the light.

A few weeks ago at lunch, my daughter, Ella, bit into a fried drumstick. *"This* is the bone that the chicken had in her leg," she said, chewing contemplatively. "That chicken or hen used to *walk* on this leg." Ella demonstrated by waving the gnawed bone across the table like a trotting bird.

I was agog. I wanted to hear what I imagine normal mothers hear when their children say something so out-of-the-mouths-of-babes true that it makes them weak. I wanted to listen to my daughter, maybe have a conversation about food choices, and I did, but I also made a note on the back of the water bill. By the time Ella got to her real point—"How does the chicken feel? Dead? What does it feel like to be *dead?"*—I was writing the scene in my head.

I can't help it. I have always used my life as material for my work, and now my children *are* my life. The memoir I'm finishing now engages the inextricable subjects of motherhood and fear, and I wonder how I'll be answering that question: *How did your family react?* I can't know until I arrive there, just as I won't know the answer to Ella's question until it's too late for me to report back.

"The chicken can't feel anything," I said. "When the chicken is dead, she doesn't feel anything at all."

"But how *does it feel to be dead?"* Ella enunciated each word in super slo-mo, hoping to nudge her dense mother toward a real answer.

"I don't know," I confessed. "Nobody knows, because once you're dead, you can't come back and tell anyone about how it felt to be dead." Then I added a nonanswer, because I was completely out of material, and even I was unsatisfied with what I'd come up with so far: "Death is one of life's great mysteries."

Ella frowned. "The farmer knows," she told me, nodding her head up and down sagely. "The farmer knows because all his chickens are *dead."*

Every spring I visit a local high school where the students in a life-writing class have read my memoir, and every spring one of these smart kids asks me a question that no adult has ever asked me, a much harder version of the The Question. "What are you going to do when your kids grow up? Are you going to let them read *Darkroom*?"

First, I make a joke about gathering up all the copies in the world and burning them, and then I answer seriously. My answer is yes, I will let my children read *Darkroom*, and then we will talk about it, but I never know what to say about when this reading will take place, or how I will prepare my children, and the question always makes the hair on the back of my neck stand up. I don't miss my opportunity in that room full of smart, sensitive sixteen-year-olds. "What would you do?" I ask them. "If I were *your* mother, what would you want me to do?"

And then I listen.

Sally Could Delete
Whatever She Wanted

PAUL AUSTIN

When I was writing a book about the way my job as an emergency room doctor almost wrecked my family, my wife and I had the following agreement: I could write whatever I wanted, and she could delete whatever she wanted. No apology, no explanation. This allowed me to write without restraint, while preserving a marriage that has sustained me for twenty-seven years. We have always made our decisions together: whether we have another child, where we will live, which job I should take. I trust her with our checkbook and our children; why would I not trust her with my writing?

I've read articles in *Poets & Writers* and other magazines in which some memoirists seem hesitant to ask a spouse or sibling about a point they're hazy on. But I'm an ER doc. And if I'm not sure that I remember the correct dose of a drug, I look it up, or I ask a nurse, or one of the other docs. Doesn't take but a second. I would hope my own doctor would do the same. I have the same expectation of my electrician: if he isn't sure that a fourteen-gauge wire is heavy enough for the circuit going to our room addition, I want him to ask someone. I wouldn't want to wake up to a house full of fire just because someone whose expertise I trusted failed to double-check an important detail.

Of course, my arrangement with Sally hinged on trust. *Something for the Pain: One Doctor's Account of Life and Death in the ER* has several chapters about the stress I carried home from work, and the corrosive effect it had on our family. It wasn't "my story," or "her story."

It was "our story." And if I planned to snap open the curtains of our living room, and toss back the covers of our bed, I thought it was only fair to give Sally a red pen, to mark through things she wouldn't want her mother, or our children, to see.

Speaking of our children, they didn't get to vote. And that brings up a difficult question: Is it possible to write about our children ethically? Are they able to give permission? In the emergency room, I always obtain informed consent prior to performing a risky procedure. Before I stick a three-inch needle in a patient's back to drain off cerebral spinal fluid, I make sure the patient understands the dangers and benefits of the procedure. And before I give someone a sedative so I can pull a dislocated shoulder back into place, I explain that the medicine may cause him to quit breathing. The patient signs his name at the bottom of a piece of paper, documenting that he thoroughly understands that the procedure may harm, rather than help him. If it's a child, the mother or father signs.

I've told our children, Sarah, John, and Sam, that they're in the book, and they don't seem to care one way or the other. I've read to John and Sam the passages in which they appear. With Sarah, it was different. She has Down syndrome. She will never read the book. She is twenty years old and lives in a group home, surrounded by caring people. I can't imagine the circumstance in which someone would say something harmful to her, after reading my book. But there are passages in the book that would hurt her, if she could read them. Should I have left those passages out? I could've limited my writing to stories about our plucky, cute, loving daughter—all of those qualities are abundantly present. I could fill a book with heart-warming lessons that my wife and I learned about unconditional love—we've learned a lot. But the fact is, our marriage took a hit. So did my expectation that life would be fair. To leave that out would be false.

And there may be a dad somewhere with a daughter with Down syndrome, and he may read the book and gain some comfort knowing that he wasn't the first father to feel disappointed that his daughter would never read beyond a sixth-grade level. Some mother may gain peace, knowing that she wasn't the only person who had worried that the family photos would always include one child who looked painfully out of place. It's painful to admit to such superficial feelings, but it would be dishonest to deny them.

In any event, I never asked my children's permission to write about them: to have done so would only have given me a false sense of fair play. When I started writing, they were eight, ten, and fourteen years old. Asking their "permission" to include them in the book would have been doubly deceitful: they were not old enough to really understand what they would be agreeing to, and if they had given their approval as children, it would have weakened their ability to object later, as adults, to having had parts of their childhoods made public. And if I'm going to write about them, it's only fair to give them the opportunity to confront me—ten, fifteen, twenty years from now—with what I've written and how it's affected them.

Since it wasn't possible to grant veto power to the children, I asked Sally to keep their interests at heart when she read the book. My therapist also does family counseling, and he read it as an advocate for Sarah, John, and Sam. As they mature, our children will doubtlessly have clear ideas about the ways in which Sally and I have succeeded and failed as parents. My book may embarrass or hurt them in ways I have not anticipated. But I'm afraid I have made other blunders that will hurt them more than including them in my book: things I've said or not said, decisions I have made that are absurdly unfair.

In the end, Sally didn't veto anything. Maybe she's braver than I am, or less concerned about what other people think. Or maybe she felt as if she came off pretty well in what I wrote. The primary arc of the book shows how I lost part of my compassion as I went through medical training, and the way in which the sleep deprivation of working the night shift uncovered a harsher, less loving side to my personality. Illuminating Sally's shortcomings, or those of our children, was never my objective: they can write their own books for that.

W. W. Norton published the book in 2008. The *Boston Globe* called it "a stunning account of the chaos of the emergency room," and *Library Journal* gave it a starred review. I would love to see it go into a second printing. But in thirty years, if I'm still alive, I'll be eighty-five years old and my book will doubtlessly be out of print. If Sally and I are in good health, we'll be in a retirement center; if in poor health, a nursing home. But wherever we are, we will have a book-shelf, and *Something for the Pain* will be on it. Of course, when Sarah, John, or Sam comes to visit, each will bring his or her own memories with them. If they notice the book at all, I hope they will forgive the flaws in the way I've told our story. But in a deeper, more vital way, I hope they'll forgive my failings as a father.

Case by Case

When It Comes to Family You Still Have to Talk To

MIMI SCHWARTZ

When the acquisitions editor called to say, "I love the manuscript, but I love your husband even more!" I thought, *Really?* The times that I called Stu a moron, or implied it, in 230 pages of my marriage memoir didn't faze her. I was glad. Our marriage was one I hoped to stay in, though hardly the perfect union, not even in year 1. I wanted to capture its ups, downs, and arounds in a story I wasn't calling fiction. I wanted to show how after so many years "[m]aybe we stay together because when I see dying grass, he sees green; when he gets faint at the sight of blood, I get Band-Aids. Or because we both like peanut butter when we're on diets. He takes a little, then I take a little, then we grin in communal sin, vowing tomorrow will be different . . ." (from *Thoughts from a Queen-sized Bed*).

Stu was also pleased. He loved having a woman in Nebraska loving him (and pushed for Paul Newman playing him in the movie), but even without fantasy, he told me, after reading the whole manuscript, "You got us right! That's how we are." The mix of tension, nurturing, joking, and ambivalence felt real to him.

Stu had seen parts of early drafts, often before two cups of morning coffee, the supreme sacrifice for him (another reason to like him). But he hadn't read our fight over who forgot the map on a trip to Cape Cod, or about struggles with monogamy, or the day of his mother's funeral. So to hear that his main objections were "I never read *Fortune* magazine" and "Take out the part about my putting chocolate syrup on cornflakes at night" was a great relief. (Yes, he gave his permission for that revelation now.)

Kim Barnes, in a *Fourth Genre* interview, said she worried about showing *In the Wilderness* to her father. It is a coming-of-age memoir about breaking away from the family's Pentecostal religion, and she had expected his fury and great hurt. To her surprise, his main complaints were, like Stu's, small details, easy to accommodate. That's when she realized: "One thing that we always assume, wrongly, is that if we write about people honestly, they will resent it and become angry. If you come at it for the right reasons and you treat people as you would your fictional characters—you know, you don't let them become static—if you treat them with complexity and compassion, sometimes they will feel as if they've been honored, not because they're presented in some ideal way but because they're presented with understanding."

These assurances, which I read halfway through writing my manuscript, became my touchstone for honesty about sharing a bed for the long haul.

The sections I'd shown Stu early on were about our major crisis: in year 20, two weeks apart, he had a heart attack and I had breast cancer. We were forty-seven and forty-eight. The six months following became what we started calling "our recuperative honeymoon," and those early morning drafts were part of our healing, individually and as a couple. They offered some permanence during a time of fragility; our inchoate hope was that no matter what, we would last on the page. The drafts also became springboards for conversation that helped a drifting marriage onto more emotionally solid ground. I started to see our life his way, something I hadn't done enough of—too busy? too self-absorbed?—and I revealed to him a vulnerability I never dared to before. Softly, softly (no yelling because of his heart), we talked, cried, hugged, and bargained over our versions of history. *That's not how I saw it! But what about . . . ? Did you really?* I never let him edit my feelings—that wasn't the point—but I did let him make his case on the page. Once, I gave him a tape recorder to tell his version of an event as if he were a stranger, and always I relied on dialogue to empower him. My rule of thumb became: When I called him a moron, he (mostly) got to call me a jerk.

So why didn't I show him everything early on? Because I had learned the hard way about the dangers of showing too much before, as Bret Lott says, "you have challenged your own first assumptions." Family members, in particular, press powerful emotional buttons that seduce us into childlike oversimplifications: "my perfect grandmother" "my hateful sister" "my selfish husband." It takes, I've found, many drafts *over time* to help test my initial emotions (usually angry, overly enthusiastic, or self-righteous) to see how well those gut responses hold up. When I wait, one-dimensional figures get fleshed out, my writing becomes more nuanced, and family members keep talking to me.

At least, the reasonable family members like Stu—and my kids and mother (whose eyesight was bad for reading). But my sister Ruth is not reasonable, I decided on the day I was to mail my manuscript off in 2001. I had stopped at the library to look up legal concerns for an article on memoir and read in Carol Meyer's *The Writer's Survival Manual*: "Even if what you say is true, you can be sued for invasion of privacy, especially under the false-light and embarrassing facts concepts." By "false-light" she meant embellishing, fictionalizing, or distorting certain facts, and "the embarrassing facts concept" meant revealing information the person has not given you permission to reveal. *That covered everything!* I immediately imagined my sister in one of her furies, dialing her lawyer. She had none of Stu's calm and inner confidence—and she hated me these days. I made the first U-turn for home and called my editor to say I'd send in the manuscript next week. I got to work.

I left Ruth as the one who battled my father for both of us. She would like herself in that part:

It was my sister Ruth who took on the serious training of a Teutonic father. The battles started when I was four and she was twelve and lasted until she married at nineteen. No, she couldn't wear lipstick. No, she couldn't stay out until midnight. . . .

"But Dad, everyone is . . ."

"You should date the Schulzberger boy. His mother is a Tannhauser and in Germany . . ."

"Dad, this is America."

But in the story of my mother's eighty-fifth birthday weekend, she had to go away. She was a disaster that weekend, driving my family, especially me, crazy. So much so that in a post-weekend journal entry, I began: "Ruth could drive anyone insane, no wonder her husband jumped off a roof. She'd make anyone do that. And no wonder her daughter ended up dead."

Really vicious stuff for pages—and nothing I planned to use (except maybe in fiction). Instead, I started telling friends about the birthday weekend and found myself saying that, thanks to my sister, the only thing I heard out of everyone's mouth was that Alan (my son) should have rented a car. "It was like a mantra!" Then I'd laugh. By the fifteenth telling, I realized that I had a way into writing the story. Same material, same people. But now I had humor to handle the anger, giving me the emotional hook and distancing I'd been missing.

Humor has often bailed me out, not just for writing about family, but for living in one. I'd say that marriage depends on it. But humor wasn't going to be enough, I knew, to save me from my sister's wrath. So she became Cousin Dora.

I knew the conversation that had gone on all day, probably all week. My mother complaining to Cousin Dora, who complained to my aunt Lisa, who told my cousin Margo, who shook her head, called for a limo, and said what would be the weekend mantra: "Alan should have rented a car." After all—and I could hear everyone, but especially Cousin Dora (the former bad girl, now family saint) on the phone for hours on this—it is Aunt Gerda's car, she should have a right to drive in it, and to pay for a limo, on her eighty-fifth birthday, no less, and with her treating everyone. It's just like Mimi and her family. She always was a spoiled brat.

I already had a disclaimer in the book: "To protect the privacy of friends and relatives I've changed names and some locations, but the rest is true—as I see it." So my pact with the reader felt secure. Switching Ruth to Dora was within the boundaries of memoir that I'd set up. True, the cousin I was thinking of didn't stir up this kind of family trouble; she simply liked wild parties, always had (a subject amply discussed in many family phone marathons). I was sure she'd know I meant Ruth, the whole family would. So I braced for Ruth's anger, but no lawsuit—and mailed the manuscript off.

Ruth called about a month after the book came out, and to my amazement, said, "I really like it, especially the part about Dad!" I never thought I'd hear any compliment from her, the last one I remember being when I swam across Lake Cayuga at camp, when I was eight and she was sixteen. A few cousins also called with congratulations, and no one sounded insulted by my satirical pokes. I had bet that they'd think I meant the others, never themselves, and I was right. Only one even asked, "Dora is Ruth, right?" No one—friends, family, or strangers—seemed to care much about the changed names, justifying a decision I had made years back about real life subjects: if someone is neither famous nor infamous, and you can use a disclaimer instead of real names, do it.

A curious thing happened when Ruth morphed into Cousin Dora. The writing got better. A sharp edge that wasn't working became rounded as my ridicule and fury softened. Ruth/Dora became more believable, more complex and nuanced, and . . . more like my sister. At least, some form of my sister, the one from Camp Inawood days, who could be generous as well as infuriating. Until Dora stepped in as mediator between past and present, I had forgotten that sister.

Annie Dillard warns against writing memoir for revenge. "While literature is an art, it is not a martial art . . . no place to defend yourself from an attack, real or imagined, and no place to launch an attack." That is a good bit of advice, but one I often have to trick myself into remembering. The more ways, the better, I've found. Humor, dialogue, letting it rest over time, changing names, whatever works for who is to be in my spotlight—and when I have to see them again.

At Its Center

PAUL LISICKY

When I'm writing about anyone I know, be it a family member, a friend, or the landscaper down the street, it's pretty much a given that I'm taking a few traits and putting borders around them, with the assumption that we all know that no story can fully capture human character in all of its range, strangeness, and unpredictability. Vivian Gornick says something similar, but in a different way. When one of her readers registers confusion that Gornick isn't quite like the speaker of *Fierce Attachments*, she replies that she and her real-life mother are "rough drafts" of their written selves.

I should also say that I can't write about somebody without tricking myself into thinking that she's in sync with the project. Maybe that's because I grew up in a family that wasn't terribly invested in old-fashioned ideas of privacy. We cared about art. But we also cared about show business and social aspiration. We wanted to be seen. Which meant that none of us felt so self-serious that we thought our experiences were ours to own and keep. When my mother said, "Are you writing about me?" she said it because she wanted me to. She wanted to believe that she mattered. Maybe she was naïve to assume that every story or description would please her, but her need to be known and present in some stranger's imagination seemed to trump that concern.

Not everyone shares that belief. I'm thinking about one relative's reaction to my memoir *Famous Builder*. Of course, the unhappiness didn't come from the aunt my brothers and I used to compare to Eva Braun; they came from the aunt I described as my second mother. That's directly from the book: "I love my Aunt C. She's like a second mother to me."

What was there not to like? I didn't get it. I could think of any number of people who might have taken offense at something I said about them—my high school music teacher; another ex, who got all of two sentences in the book—but Aunt C.? But mad she was, so mad that she couldn't talk to me about it. So she talked to her daughter, who talked to my mother, who talked to my brother, who called me to say, *Now look at the mess you made.*

And years later, the fire still burns.

It's too easy to be irritated with her for involving my family in her objections, for refusing to draw the line between life and art, but as soon as I think like that, I cringe. Who's in power here? The truth is, someone in Aunt C.'s situation is entitled to her say, even if she's only a minor character in the book. She never thought of herself as a minor character. And maybe that was the most shocking thing about finding herself, unrecognizable, on the pages of her nephew's book: the world could go on without her at its center.

The portrait of my Aunt C. revolves around the time she was taking care of my grandmother, who must have been suffering with Alzheimer's, though no one called it that back then. I'm not sure why that task fell entirely to Aunt C., given that she had six living siblings, but she took her mother into her house, even as she was raising three young children. I think of her packing my cousins' lunches and changing her mother's diaper within minutes. I think of her guiding her mother up the stairs by her elbow while her youngest is tugging at the hem of her skirt. It's hard not to wonder, in retrospect, how unnerving it must have felt for her to see the major story of her life concentrated in an anecdote. In my book I use the stories around my grandmother's illness to talk about how my father felt torn between his attachment to his mother and his need to be on his own. I use them to point to the collision between his drive for achievement and the immigrant rituals of his siblings who stayed on in working-class

Pennsylvania. Then there's that scene where my father writes a check to Aunt C. She refuses it, and it's literally thrown back and forth for ten minutes, until she pushes it in her pocket, accepting it, finally, as both a matter of winning and defeat.

It would be foolish to expect Aunt C. to read that exchange simply through the constricted lens of theme. How was she reconstructing that memory in her imagination? And what did she know that I didn't? For me the scene was only there to illustrate my father's guilt and gratitude, but what humiliations lay beyond the words I'd put on the page?

Now that my own mother has dementia, it's not exactly possible not to write about it. Even when I'm trying to describe, say, the knife on the dining room table or the sun striking a tree trunk, I'm writing about my mother and her loss of identity. Which makes me wonder: how will that writing play out among my siblings one day? The lesson is obvious but simple: we have absolutely no control over how others interpret our work, even when we think we're writing out of affection. Sometimes I remember that old family of ours, and what it was like to have an easy conversation without feeling we had to tiptoe around something so much larger than us.

CODA

My mother dies. Aunt C. is at the funeral. As luck would have it, Aunt C. sits across from me at the restaurant after the service. The palms shine beside the dunes outside the window. We talk and we laugh with an ease that suggests the book was never written.

The Day I Cried at Starbucks

RUTH BEHAR

It could've been blissful, my four-month visit to Miami Beach in 2009 to escape the dreariness of a Michigan winter. I was on my own. David was teaching in Michigan and Gabriel had already graduated from NYU and was living in Brooklyn. I'd rented an apartment in a historic Art Deco building a block from the ocean. As soon as I got organized, I planned to invite my uncle Miguel and aunt Reina and their children and grandchildren, as well as my mother's cousin Anna, for Sunday brunch so they could admire the lovely view.

But in February, a gorgeous time of the year in Miami, an essay I'd published in *Hadassah Magazine* demolished my family plans.

Originally, I'd given the piece an innocuous title, "The Yiddish Book from Cuba." I told the story of how, with Baba's help, I'd come into the possession of my great-grandfather's handwritten memoir. "I'm glad we were such good thieves," I'd written.

The editor at *Hadassah Magazine* saw the dramatic potential of this line and changed the title of my essay to "Such Good Thieves." I feared the new title would be misunderstood and read as a statement of fact by my family and tried to change it back to the old one. But it was too late. The magazine had already gone to press.

It was my first time publishing in *Hadassah Magazine*. Just before her death, Baba had made me a life member of Hadassah, a Jewish women's organization in which she'd been active after retiring and

Note: Some names have been changed to protect the privacy of family members.

settling in Miami Beach. I thought it would be nice to honor her by publishing my essay in the organization's widely circulated magazine.

What I hadn't anticipated was that "widely circulated" meant that my family, as well as many friends of my family who form part of the Cuban Jewish immigrant circle, saw the essay. Worst of all, they actually read it. And they hated it.

Among those who hated it most was my uncle Miguel.

He phoned me and said, "Can you meet me at the Starbucks on Lincoln Road tomorrow morning?"

"Sure, okay."

"Eleven o'clock. I've got to talk to you about your article in *Hadassah Magazine*."

My uncle was asking me to meet him at Starbucks? I didn't remember any occasion when I'd been alone with him. My aunt Reina was always with him. Often their three children and their spouses and grandchildren were also around. They're a tight-knit family and live within a few blocks of each other in Miami Beach.

Miguel was the baby; my aunt Sylvia was ten and my mother was eight when he was born. The family had just moved to Havana from Agramonte. By a stroke of good fortune, Zayde had won 5,000 pesos in the Cuban lottery in 1944. With that money he and Baba were able to move from the countryside and buy their lace shop on Calle Aguacate.

When I was born, Miguel was twelve—too young to be an uncle.

There's a yellowed photograph I keep in a frame above my desk in Michigan. I'm a year old, decked out in a sailor dress and perched on Zayde's lap in the balcony of our old apartment in La Habana. Mami sits in the rocking chair next to us. Miguel balances on the arm of Mami's chair. In his short-sleeved shirt and tailored pants, he's no longer a boy, but neither is he yet a man.

Afterward, when we all left Cuba and settled in the United States, I felt that my uncle Miguel didn't approve of the kind of woman I'd become—too intellectual, too independent, too liberal. I was married and a mother, yet I traveled by myself on return journeys to Cuba, a place we weren't supposed to go back to.

"I didn't realize there was a Starbucks on Lincoln Road," I say.

"It's there. You'll find it."

I hear a jittery edge to his voice.

The next morning, a Sunday, I'm up early and take a walk on the beach, enjoying the ocean's calm, the breeze like silk against my skin. The sun warms my shoulders. I feel lucky. It's icy back in Michigan.

But I don't linger. I want to be punctual for my appointment with Miguel. My parking spot turns out to be around the corner from the Starbucks I'd never noticed. All the tables outside are taken, so I claim a table inside, next to the window. I toss the leftover paper cups and wipe the table with a napkin. Then I busy myself deleting spam on my BlackBerry.

The phone rings.

"Are you there?"

"Yes, but no rush. Take your time."

"I'll be there soon. I just wanted to be sure you were there."

Miguel arrives, and our cheeks brush against each other as we quickly kiss hello. It stuns me to think he's in his midsixties. My young uncle. His cheeks are redder, his thinning hair grayer.

"What do you want to drink?" he asks.

"I'll take an iced tea."

"Iced tea in the morning? Not coffee?"

"I don't drink coffee in the morning. It gives me migraines."

By Miguel's frown I see that my reply reinforces his idea of me as an oddball.

He returns and places the cup in front of me. "It's passion fruit tea. Is that okay?"

"Thanks, that's great."

He's gotten a large coffee for himself. He reaches into his shirt pocket and unfolds a ragged photocopy of my essay.

I wince when I see it.

"You're ready?" Miguel says.

"Sure, shoot."

I look at his copy stabbed with underlining and highlighting. It's almost illegible.

"Here, at the beginning, you say you're a scholar and that's why you deserved to inherit The Book my grandfather wrote. But what's a scholar? A scholar's somebody who knows a lot about a subject. I'm an accountant because I know a lot about accounting. I'm a scholar too. I'm a scholar of accounting. So I should have The Book. Are you going to give it to me?"

Before I can think of how to reply, he takes a pen from his shirt pocket and circles a word that's already been circled.

"This, I really hated. 'Tiny.' Why'd you use that word?"

"You mean my referring to Baba and Zayde's lace store in Havana as tiny?"

"It wasn't tiny. It wasn't any smaller than the other stores owned by Jews on Calle Aguacate."

"But I'm not comparing their store to anybody else's store. I'm just saying *their* store was tiny. That's what I always heard."

"How do you know? You're not old enough to remember. I remember. I was there. I worked with them in the store. And then Castro came and took it away."

"Would you have preferred if I'd said 'small' instead of 'tiny'?"

"Maybe. 'Tiny' makes their store sound poor—like it was nothing. Like they were nobody."

"I'm sorry. I didn't realize you could read so much into the word 'tiny.' I was just saying their store was a very small store."

"You're supposed to be a writer, but you don't seem to think about the meaning of the words you're using."

I glance out the window, enviously taking in the profane beauty of a Sunday on Lincoln Road: translucent morning light, swaying palm trees, people strolling along the pedestrian boulevard, looking marvelously carefree, clasping their children, their exotic dogs, their trophy shopping bags, their lovers.

With his pen Miguel recircles another word.

"Then you say that Baba worked at a 'rundown store' when we came to New York. It wasn't rundown. Do you know whose store that was? It belonged to Jacobo. He was a friend of the family. You think he'd like you saying his store was 'rundown'? That's not a nice thing to say."

"But the store *was* rundown! That I do remember. I used to go help Baba and Zayde on Saturdays. I remember Gem Fabrics. I remember how the elevated train rattled above the store. I remember how Baba wore scissors tied on a string around her neck, the scissors for cutting fabric."

"It was a good store. Jacobo was very nice to give them jobs. I worked there too. I worked very hard. I had to carry packages to the storeroom. We didn't have any money and I had to help out. You probably don't know that."

I envision Miguel at seventeen, newly arrived from Cuba, scarcely able to speak English, and having to spend his days lugging bundles and bolts of fabric, his eyes itchy from the dust, his hands sore and calloused. In those days he lived with Baba and Zayde in their one-bedroom apartment in Queens, two flights below our apartment, and before dinner, as was the custom in Cuba, he'd take a shower. I remember him in a big bath towel as he sprang from the bathroom to the bedroom, leaving a trail of talcum powder, white as glistening sand.

Miguel skims the next couple of lines. Fortunately, he doesn't see anything offensive. Then his pen stops at the point where I state that The Book fell into the hands of my great-uncle Moshe. Attacking the line with a glob of black ink, he reads my own words aloud to me: "This wasn't surprising; he'd done well for himself, both in Cuba and Miami, and reigned over the family as a respected godfather."

"This is horrible. How could you call him a 'godfather'? A godfather is a mafioso, someone who kills others to get what he wants."

"I wasn't using the word that way! I was thinking of *padrino* in the Cuban or Latin American sense—as the patriarch, the head of the family."

"You said 'godfather.' You really hurt Anna's feelings with that word."

Anna, my second cousin, is Moshe's only surviving child. She too lives in Miami Beach but refrained from calling or meeting me in person. Instead, she sent me an e-mail to let me know how upset she was about my essay. She commanded me never to write about her father again. "Let him rest in peace," she insisted. But at the end of the e-mail she wrote, "I still love you." I wasn't sure she meant it, though. She later told other members of the family that she doesn't want to see me again.

I feel bad about hurting Anna's feelings. My heart has always gone out to her. Her younger brother died of leukemia in Cuba, and while he was dying, no one told her what was going on. I've written about searching for his Jewish grave in Cuba, and though I've done so in the most tender way I could, she told me in her e-mail that she didn't want me to write about her brother anymore either.

Miguel shakes his head. "Anna didn't want her children to see your essay. She knew they'd be angry. But someone saw it in California and sent it to her daughter."

Anna also has two sons. I've always gotten along well with them, especially her younger son, who has an artistic soul and bears the namesake of her brother. Maybe he too has vowed not to speak to me anymore.

But what can I do about the fact that in Cuba, and in our Cuban Jewish enclave, Moshe *was* the godfather of the family? We all depended on his largesse. It was Moshe who gave my newlywed father, a Sephardic Jew who'd grown up in a tenement near the Port of Havana, an accounting job at his store so he could properly support my mother, who fell pregnant (with me) the instant she married. It was Moshe who sold one of his condominiums to Baba and Zayde when they headed south to Miami Beach for their final years of sunshine. It was Moshe who supported his younger brother, Jaime, a dreamer and a socialist, and his four nieces on Kibbutz Gaash in Israel.

Did I mean to suggest Moshe was evil because he was a man of means and knew that he was? Not for a moment. I found him to be very charming and we got along well. He was forever asking why I didn't go dig up something in Israel. I'd tell him I wasn't an archaeologist, and he'd say that didn't matter. He thought it was great that I loved doing research, and he hoped I'd write one day about the history of the Jews of Cuba. Once, when I was visiting Miami, he led me on a wild-goose chase for supposedly important documents that we tracked down in some old suitcases in a friend's warehouse. The "documents" turned out to be mostly clippings from the social pages of Miami newspapers that were barely legible; they had gotten waterlogged in a flood and turned to mush. We had a roller-coaster adventure searching for them all over the city, with Moshe bringing his Cadillac to a full stop on the highway several times to be able to read the exit signs. It was truly a miracle we didn't end up in a car crash. But I was touched by Moshe's desire to help me with my research. In retrospect, I think going on this hapless quest for nonexistent historical documents is my fondest memory of him.

I could understand why his daughter and grandchildren would find my portrait of him in my essay unbecoming. They'd depict Moshe as the big-hearted philanthropist of the family. Being at a distance, and coming from the poorer side, I picked up on the resentment that the recipients of his largesse, particularly my father and grandfather, came to feel; I picked up on the way Baba seemed to admire her brother more than her husband, my beloved Zayde; I picked up on the way Mami seemed not to notice that Papi still carried wounds from the days he'd been treated by Moshe as merely a poor *turco*, and that was the reason he demanded obedience and ruled in our house with the power of a little dictator. A generation later, I hadn't escaped the "hidden injuries of class." I was ashamed. In a world where worth is measured by wealth, those closest to me had not been able to achieve enough. "Empty pockets don't ever make the grade," as Billie Holiday sang so heart wrenchingly. And I was foolish enough to think I could make it up to Zayde and Papi with my writing.

Miguel, I soon learned, had no sympathy for my position. "Did it ever occur to you that maybe Moshe had The Book for a reason? He was the eldest son. Maybe his father wanted him to have it."

"I really don't think so. Baba was the eldest child."

"But you don't know for sure."

"No, I don't."

"And so you decided to turn your grandmother—my mother—into a thief, so you could get The Book for yourself."

"I didn't force Baba to do anything. I suggested that she keep The Book, but she was free to do whatever she wanted."

"She loved you so much she would've done anything for you."

"And I would've done anything for her. I adored Baba."

"Then why did you stain her name?"

"I didn't stain her name."

"You did. You say she was a 'good thief.' There's one thing my father always said: the most important possession a person has in life in his name. If you ruin that, you ruin everything."

"Miguel, please! I used 'thief' as a metaphor."

"Look, what I think you forget is that Baba didn't belong just to you. She was also my mother. She was also my children's grandmother. We all loved her—not just you."

These words inexplicably bring tears to my eyes.

Miguel smiles. "Good," he says. "It's good you're crying."

He keeps his gaze on me and I feel so humbled I lower my head. When I finally look up, I see a long line of people waiting to be served at the counter. How I wish I could dissolve into that crowd and never be heard from again.

But the knife cuts deeper. "You're the kind of scholar who'd do anything to get the documents you want, aren't you? What would you think if I called your university in Michigan and told them you stole The Book from your great-uncle because you thought you had a right to it? And you don't even read Yiddish! So why are you keeping it?"

"Miguel, I was the only one who ever cared about the history of the family. So what if I have the original? You can read the story. It's all been translated."

"What if I want to be the one who's got the original? Will you give The Book to me? Or do I have to go steal it out of your file cabinet?"

I want to say, "Sure, I'll give you The Book if you want it so badly." But those words refuse to come out of my mouth. As I take the last sip of my passion fruit tea, I'm convinced I'm the lowest of the low. I expect Miguel to rip up my essay before my eyes. But he folds it neatly, this writing of mine to which he'd devoted Talmudic atten-

tion, and stuffs it back into his shirt pocket. We say good-bye polite-
ly, walking our separate ways on Lincoln Road.

The days pass. I never miss a morning's walk on the beach.

I don't hear from Miguel or my aunt Reina. Nor do I phone them.

Two of my mother's cousins come for a visit in April, and they
meet separately with me for lunch on Lincoln Road. They tell me
about the family dinner at Little Havana Restaurant. Anna, as well
as Miguel and Reina, refuse to go if I'm going.

Passover, the Jewish remembrance of our freedom from slavery,
comes and goes. I remain in exile—unworthy of a place at the seder
table.

Near the end of my time in Miami Beach, in early May, I'm driving on the Venetian causeway that leads back to my rental apartment,
and I catch a fleeting glimpse of Miguel and Reina taking a sunset
walk.

Evenings are growing hot already. I watch Miguel wipe his brow
with a handkerchief. Reina stands next to him patiently. They've been
sweethearts since she was thirteen and he was fifteen in Cuba. I hope
they'll always be blessed, my young uncle, my affable aunt, who loves
to sing and is the life of every party. In the past, I would've stopped
the car and turned back to greet them, gone home with them. But I
feel I should crawl away. I'm a stranger.

Then it's time to pack my bags and return to Michigan, where a
cold spring awaits me. Before I close the door of the Art Deco apartment, I look back at the view—the infinite sky, the turquoise ocean,
still there, still so beautiful.

At that moment, I don't know yet that eventually my uncle Miguel
will forgive me and I will be welcome again in the warmth of his and
Reina's home. At that moment, I don't know yet that later, much
later, even my cousin Anna will take me back as family. At that moment, when I feel certain my sins are too great to ever be forgiven,
I'm grateful that the sky and the ocean still love me.

Memory Lessons

RIGOBERTO GONZÁLEZ

Like any memoirist who writes so revealingly about family, I'm inevitably asked what my family thinks about my work, which is a diplomatic way of asking how my family feels about my showing the world the intimate portraits of our household. How does my aunt sleep at night knowing one of her nephews has left the curtains open and that strangers walking by might have caught her standing in the middle of the room while wearing nothing but her old bra? Does my cousin take exception to my writer's graffiti—*My cousin is a drunk!*—on the public stalls? Does my thirty-something younger brother mind being judged for a comment he made when he was only eight years old?

The quick answer is that few members of my family can read what I write. They either don't know how to read, or they don't read English. Both my parents are now deceased, so that gives me a certain freedom from guilt, and my brother, the only member of my family who holds any interest in my work, loves to read what I write and then shake his head with disapproval—not at the fact I wrote it down, but at the flaws and follies of the past that we both remember. "Sad," my brother declares each time. "So sad."

Despite these permissions, when I initially set out to write a memoir, I did so with plenty of hesitation. First, I had few models within the Latino literary landscape to learn from. There were Esmeralda Santiago, Richard Rodriguez and Luis Alberto Urrea. I applauded their bravery, their skill at shaping memory into something bigger than themselves, but my own story seemed a little grittier—more sex, more drugs, more rock and roll. And so, I suspected, were theirs. I always thought this was the Latino writer's limitation: the inability to truly and without censorship air out the dirtiest items in the laundry basket. It's a cultural expectation: keep it within the walls of the home, honor the privacy of the living, respect the secrets of the dead.

My earliest attempts at nonfiction certainly adhere to these tenets. I wrote about my elementary school teachers, my first crush, the longing for my beloved México after migrating to California. There was a certain childlike innocence that bothered me about what I was writing because even as a child I knew more than I let on, yet here I was, pretending yet again that I didn't. But I wasn't a child anymore. I had lost my innocence a very long time ago. In fact, it had chipped away over the years: after moving to the United States and living in poverty, after enduring years of physical and verbal abuse from my grandfather, after my mother's death, after my father abandoned me, after leaving home as a teenager and never going back, after becoming involved with an abusive lover, after becoming entangled in drugs, alcohol, and the unhealthy lifestyle of many young and careless gay men. Who was I trying to kid?

I held a very different lens to the world. It was cracked and scratched, and even the prettier things in life appeared somewhat smudged. This didn't necessarily mean that I was walking the earth wrapped inside a cloud of depression—though I had my bad days; it simply meant that when I looked back to the past, when I dug through the rubble of memory, the difficult moments called out to me the loudest. Every hardship longed to be documented as evidence of my perseverance. I had lost so much, and yet I didn't feel empty-handed.

I resolved to tell it completely if I was going to speak up at all, especially because of another limitation of the Latino family: revisionist memory. When I was younger, I usually questioned my own ability to retain information, because I was prone to remembering things a little differently. When I sat down to eavesdrop on the adults talking story, I usually found myself thinking, *That's not how it happened. Did it?* But since I was only a kid, I deferred to the grown-ups and simply adjusted my own version to match theirs. This didn't happen too many times before I realized that what those grown-ups were doing was getting their stories straight. It was an exercise in communal imagination, and there were many reasons for changing a story: to protect themselves, their children, or each other; to silence fact; to demonstrate discretion; to recover dignity; to deceive; to deny and to derail previous versions. To deliberately forget was both a good and a bad practice, and it took place in my childhood home repeatedly.

Every family, I suspect, exercises this tactic for keeping the peace, if not ensuring survival. In every class, in every culture, in every corner of the world sits a little house with windows that only show what its inhabitants want to show. It's a self-imposed code of honor that keeps a semblance of "order," "normativity," and "functionality." (Yes, these are ironic quotation marks.) *Nothing alarming happens here*, the window curtains declare when they sway sleepily with the afternoon breeze. Conflict is usually small and containable—a spat over the use of the television, a disagreement about politics, a complaint about a toothpaste cap carelessly dropped into the drain. But the neighbors— now *there's* a family with problems. But not this one, not ours, not here.

I learned the art of delusion early: if a man leaves a bruise, it isn't violence, it's passion; if a woman cries in her sleep it isn't grief, it's her fragile nerves; if a child crumbles inside the anxiety of a toxic household where everyone implodes with rage, sadness, and worry, it isn't family dysfunction, it's his own sensitive nature that's to blame. Give him a cup of chamomile tea and an aspirin. Dab a thimble of alcohol onto his temples and put him to bed. Nothing's happening, boy. Go to sleep, and tomorrow, when you awake, all will be well again.

And so my childhood, and so my adolescence, keeping the family sacred while we pitied the neighbors and their unfortunate demonstrations on the front lawn: public fights and other forms of gratuitous theater. They yelled and hurled whatever they held in their hands at the moment of outburst; they honked their car horns with hostility; they stomped in and out of the house with resolve. And yet, we were all afraid to admit, they somehow also loved because they practiced something no one in our house did: affection. We saw them kiss hello and good-bye, we marveled at their habit of embracing with spontaneity and joy, even; we saw them touch each other constantly—an arm around the waist, a hand on the shoulder, a flirtatious palm against the buttocks. That was how they worked: if they were going to showcase one emotion, they were going to show them all. But in the González house: we kept everything hidden. Even displays of love. There was only one way out, and it was finite. There was only one way to look back, and that was by leaving.

Leaving home was the blessing, and even the brute that was my grandfather respected me for that, for accomplishing what no one else had done. For others, there was always the fear of getting lost, of feeling abandoned or without recourse because we were not from this country.

Since I am no longer at home, I am no longer bound to the family codes, and no longer under the pressure of my family's immediate scrutiny. And I know that what I write down is simply my version, not the definitive, unchallengeable truth. Because for something to be true, all one has to do is believe in it, and my family believes wholeheartedly the stories they spin into the family's lore. And so do I. I am now the creator of the text and therefore in control. That doesn't mean that I am the righteous one, however, or that my remembrance of things past is the most accurate. If anything, I have also learned about my shortcomings, flaws, and mistakes as a history keeper, as a story seeker and memory excavator. Let me illustrate that point with the following.

In the summer of 1981 my mother suffered a stroke at the age of thirty, which left her partially paralyzed. One side of her face was frozen in a state of perpetual sadness, and though she was able to express joy with the other side of her face, I never learned to see past the side that was falling off her skull.

To make matters worse, her ability to speak had been greatly compromised. At the height of her energy she managed only to slur;

when she tired, she was incomprehensible. And always she carried around with her a white handkerchief, which she used to wipe off the spittle that would seep out of the corner of her mouth. Even her laughter was unfamiliar, more like a hiccup than a giggle.

In any case, we learned to move through her illness and slow recovery, through the halls of the blinding white hospitals and the uncertainty of a pending surgery in which a heart valve was to be replaced. The distress paralyzed my mother even further. I knew she was scared. We all were. We had just come into this country a year before, had just begun to learn this foreign language, and now here we were, making life-changing and life-saving decisions through what little we were told and what little we understood.

Because we were unsure about whether my mother would survive the surgery, we managed a special visitors' visa for my grandparents to come from México to see their ailing daughter before she went into the operating room.

The family reunion was slightly anticlimactic. My grandparents were tired from the long journey up from Michoacán—a three-day trip by bus—and my mother's health had been deteriorating at an alarming speed. I had become a fixture in that hospital room because, at eleven years old, I had picked up more English than anyone else in the family, and I stuttered my way through a communication between my father and the hospital staff. There were a few bilingual nurses floating around, but they were in such great demand that we scarcely saw them, so we had to make do with what we had: me.

There we were, my mother, my grandparents and me, silent and immobile among the unfamiliar contraptions—tubes and lights and metallic boxes—yet another language we did not know in that American hospital. By this time, my mother could no longer speak and I could tell she wanted to say something to my grandparents. They had been holding each other, and kissing and comforting one another with caresses, but that was not enough. My mother had something more to say—a wish, a request, a demand—something. So she resorted to the unthinkable—to writing it down. You see, with only a first-grade education, my mother's writing skills were limited. My grandparents, with no education, couldn't read or write at all. But an effort was made. My mother, fueled by a sense of desperation, wrote a sentence across a piece of paper and showed it to my grandparents.

We were all stunned. My mother knew her parents couldn't read. Since I had been the go-between all this time I thought that maybe I could help and read the sentence for them. But imagine my surprise at the illegible scribble before me. It was neither English nor Spanish. It was a squiggly, loopy design, but it meant something to my mother. She had written something important on that piece of paper.

I knew then that at that moment any one of us could have broken the spell, but through some communal sense of intuition, none of us did. I kept my mouth shut about not being able to read what had been written, and my grandparents considered that scribble thoughtfully, and then nodded their heads. "We understand, Avelina," my grandmother told my mother. "We understand."

Over the years, after moving through the fifth anniversary of my mother's death, then the tenth, the fifteenth, and more recently, the twenty-sixth, I went back to that moment and the curiosity got to me—what was it that my grandparents had understood? Did they actually decipher something out of that scribble? Was it a symbol and not a string of words that had been drawn on that piece of paper? Or was it something else entirely that they had understood? Were they simply humoring my mother, or were they actually connecting with her in some mysterious way?

I have asked my grandmother three times about it, and each time there has been a different answer. The first time she said that my mother had thanked them for making the long journey north, and that she had asked them to look after my brother and me, should she not survive the surgery. For a long time afterward I believed the first part; the second part, I concluded, was simply my grandmother's wishful thinking.

The next time I asked her, my grandmother admitted that there was nothing comprehensible about that script, and that she had simply pretended, hoping that my grandfather had understood, come to find out later that he hadn't either, so they too were left puzzled by the gesture and by the statement scribbled in pencil. They had pondered it very briefly, and then never discussed it again.

But the third time I brought up that incident, my grandmother, perhaps unwilling to revisit that day anymore, simply said she didn't remember. When I became persistent and tried to jog her memory, she grew frustrated and then eventually cried out, "What does it matter anymore? All I have left is the shame that your mother asked us for something and we never understood what it was!"

And then she burst into tears. And then I burst into tears because as a child I knew when to keep my mouth shut, but as an adult I didn't know any better—because, after all this time, I had finally broken the spell of that incident and its memory by overthinking it, overanalyzing it, overscrutinizing it beneath the microscope of curiosity.

For many years after that last exchange with my grandmother, I felt guilty and slightly confused about what I had brought to the surface. In this case, my actions had hurt someone I loved. And it made me reflect about my literary pursuits and this fascination I had: writing about my family. It made me wonder whether it was wrong, putting my recollections into print. I knew it was unlikely that my immediate aunts, uncles and cousins would ever read them—but their children and grandchildren might. Was it fair, this glimpse into their family's past through someone else's subjective mind? Sadly, I don't have an answer, just the impulse to write it down.

All these years I have been writing it down. It is how I turn anecdote into meaning and story into significance. It is another way of remembering. And for me, it is also a way to recover what I no longer have—my parents, my childhood—and to reconstruct the broken days of my past. And in the process of building and rebuilding, I have learned an art. And like any art, memory and memoir is meant to go public, no matter how personal, no matter how small.

I am no more important than before I wrote it down, though perhaps I am a little wiser about what I have been through. It has become more real—no, it is not the truth, it is experience—human, imperfect, and beautiful. Why then must I justify writing down what I write? Why then am I frequently asked to apologize for the ability to remember? Why then do I get so defensive? I will no longer make excuses because I had no choice to be a witness. I am not a victim of circumstance but rather the participant in one of the many theaters of life. How will I know what role I played if I do not reflect upon it?

Butterfly Boy is my book of memories, and I know that I misremembered a few events, that I have forgotten and suppressed information, that my subconscious might have even made things up to protect myself or others—that, like Akira Kurosawa's *Rashomon*, if the other witnesses were called in to give testimony, their stories might be incongruent with mine, but would be just as valid.

Once upon a time, I even feared that members of my family would read my book and be appalled at how my eyes had seen them. But not anymore. That was me, back then. That was them, back then. And I hope they understand that my grown-up eyes see them quite differently now. I also hope they understand that this is what I do—remember—and that this is yet another way for me to love them like I could not before. And if my actions still offend them, then I hope they have the insight to do what I have been doing all along: sit down and ask, *Why?*

The Part I Can't Tell You

ARIEL GORE

On the last night of *The Traveling Death and Resurrection Show*, after my final reading and performance, my Catholic priest stepfather lay down and died.

That is, I'm afraid, all I can tell you.

Memoir is a strange genre—and God bless anyone who wants to avoid it—but it's a genre we're somehow drawn to.

Truth. Or some attempt at it.

Every season, some twenty new writers show up at the first meeting of the memoir workshop I teach. And they want to write.

They are excited.

They are afraid.

They have one question before we begin. What will happen, they want to know, if they ever do write? Worse, what will happen if they publish?

I've written a book-length memoir, dozens of short stories from real life, and several collections of autobiographical essays, so my students figure I'll be able to answer their simple questions. And I do have a couple of answers. But I have more questions, too.

Because, it turns out, I am like them.

I am excited.

I am afraid.

I want to tell my stories. I want to write the truth. But instead I hem and haw. I scrawl barely legible rants across unlined pages in my journal, and then I go to the computer and dream up a thousand reasons why I cannot tell the truth.

Like me, like everyone.

We want so much truth, but often we end up writing half-truths and outright lies because this is what we really want: we want to write a searing memoir, but we don't want it to cost us.

We're not lazy—we don't expect writing to be easy—but we want it to be *easier* than it is.

And why shouldn't we want that? Why shouldn't we expect that? Every day, we see fifty-year-olds who look like thirty-year-olds on TV talk shows, and they're making millions selling us on their own "authenticity."

Honesty is effortless, like the breeze, they promise us. The truth will set you free.

We want to be free.

But surely we don't have to tell the *whole* truth, do we? Surely we can clean our stories up a little bit. Surely we don't have to confess all the shadowed and angry details. How about a *goodly portion* of the truth? That will be enough, won't it?

I mean, it's not like we want to write some searing memoir because we want piles of money or golden shooting stars of glory—we know that most memoirs don't earn their authors much in terms of cash or credibility. Our motives are purer than that. We want to write our stories because we want what all writers want: we want to convey our naked and human heart/souls to the naked and human heart/souls of other human beings.

Simple as that.

And pure.

But here's the catch: we want that to be just a little bit easier than it is.

And so we lie.

Writing fiction isn't easy, but there's an ease to fiction. In fiction, there are certain prices we do not have to pay. Fiction is forgiving, allows us our secrets, allows us some level of dignity.

False memoir allows us our secrets, too. We can open our big, sad eyes for the portrait in the *New York Times* or on our blogs and we can say, "Look at me, I have suffered," and then we can tell our fantasized stories about foster-care gang life in south central Los Angeles or maybe how we were raised by wolves after our parents were killed in the Holocaust. *Certainly there is some big news story that will explain away the hole in my heart.* Or maybe we don't have to come up with lives *completely* other than the ones we've lived. Maybe we can just embellish a little here, omit a little there. Maybe if we spent two nights in jail we can write about our year in the penitentiary. It certainly *felt* like a year.

It's funny, because when I was a kid we all lied to each other to make our lives sound more socially acceptable than they actually were. We lied to make ourselves sound richer, whiter, more normal. I told the girl across the street that my stepfather was my real father and the crazy guy muttering to himself in the truck outside was just some stranger. "I don't know who he is. Why should I know?"

"Well, he *says* he's your father," she snapped, hands on her hips.

I rolled my eyes. "My God. You'll believe *anything.*"

"Lying was our bread and butter and our salvation," Katherine Arnoldi writes in the autobiographical short story "All for One and One for All." "We started out with nothing, threw in some lies, and came up with pure and glorious Power, which we were all into that year. Lies could give us wealth, create famous relatives, take us to Disneyland and back, turn hand-me-downs into store-bought clothes, make week-old runs in hose happen just that day, and give us father."

I lied to get out of trouble. "I didn't do it," I insisted. "I don't know why the store manager would say I stole all that Hello Kitty stationery." And then I'd back up in front of the pile of pink paper. "I don't know where all that came from."

Later, when I got to college, everyone's lies seemed upside-down. Now people lied to make themselves sound poorer, darker, more *unique*.

In college, they played oppression derby. "You think your father was bad? My father beat me twice as hard as that." And they'd raise their eyebrows real high, like, *Top that*.

"I didn't even *have* a father."

And, "You think living in the projects was rough? We lived in a cardboard *box*."

In college, I felt embarrassed that I'd never lived in a cardboard box. I'd lived in squats in Europe as a teenager, in abandoned farmhouses, but I couldn't imagine what it would be like to live in a cardboard box. I felt ashamed of my privilege, but I was still lying to clean things up.

On the last night of *The Traveling Death and Resurrection Show*, after my final reading and performance, my Catholic priest stepfather lay down and died.

For nearly two years now, I've been trying to figure out how to tell you more.

I've been trying to write about that night, that weekend. About my stepfather. He was the father I'd known, the father I grew up with, the father who was excommunicated from the Catholic Church for marrying my mother. He was the one who built the wooden playhouse in my kindergarten schoolyard, the one who taught me to paddle a canoe across a high Sierra lake, the one whose leg I clung to in the produce aisle at the Briar Patch Co-op Market. My dignified stepfather, who probably never had to clean anything up.

But the story of his death begins, quite unfortunately, at least one night before I knew he would die.

So the story-camera focuses in on me and my friends, unsuspecting. We're on candid camera. *Oh. Delete that picture, will you? Can we Photoshop that one?* I've been trying to tell this story, but I've wanted— *so badly*—to avoid the details. Why should I have to tell the whole truth, anyway? It's irrelevant, *isn't it?*

But how can I explain how I really felt—how can I convey even some small portion of my naked and human heart/soul if I cannot tell you anything of the shadowed and angry details?

When the sad-news e-mail comes, we all jump to apply our makeup. In the wake of death, we all know that this day, this weekend, this month, will be remembered. We grieve, we allow our tears to run mascara down our cheeks, we act out, squabble with our siblings— but we wear slimming black. We are raw, but we are also, somehow, on our best behavior.

The night before, we are simply caught. Off guard.

So it's the last night of the book tour for *The Traveling Death and Resurrection Show*, my novel about a Catholic-themed traveling freak show. My girlfriend and I have been touring the country putting on a theatrical adaptation of the book and we've ended up here, in Santa Fe, New Mexico.

The last show is over. The whole tour has been a great success. We've sold hundreds of books. And this last show has been the perfect ending. Packed venue and cheering applause. I've even managed to quit smoking after a pack a day for twenty years.

We're back at my girlfriend's ex-girlfriend's house now. We're drinking whiskey. I want a cigarette, but I don't smoke. Maybe I'm drinking twice as much as anyone else. But it doesn't matter. Tomorrow I will have forgotten today. Tomorrow I will have forgotten everything but the last performance, the applause and the smiles. This now is already slipping out of focus.

This is the last night of my stepfather's life, but I don't know that yet. It's no coincidence that this is the last night of my tour, but I don't know that yet, either.

Yeah, pour me another shot. Thanks.

My stepfather, it turns out, has waited patiently for my book tour to end. He didn't want to upset me while I still had shows to perform. And so here we are—my girlfriend and I—in Santa Fe, New Mexico, on the last night of my stepfather's life.

And so, yes, I'll have another drink. I need it. The show is over, and back at the house now my girlfriend and her ex-girlfriend insist on singing, over and over again, a mournful duet about two people who never should have broken up.

My girlfriend and I have been together for five years. My heart aches. But more than that, I'm embarrassed.

I am *so* planning to forget this.

An acquaintance of my girlfriend's ex-girlfriend shows up, a stranger to me, and whispers in my ear: "They don't know how bad this is." With that comment she had meant to support me, I think, to sort of squeeze my hand and offer her condolences. Instead, her words cement my humiliation.

Yes, I want another drink.

My sixteen-year-old daughter has called from New York. Away at summer art school, she has managed, somehow, to soak her cell phone, misplace her ATM card, and pierce her face. "There might be some drama here," she explains on the voicemail message.

I've spent my life savings to send her to this summer program.

And, "Well, Mom, I don't think I'm going to get kicked out. It's just . . . It's so stupid. It wasn't my fault."

She needs me to send money. And right away.

I leave my girlfriend and her ex-girlfriend to their mournful duet, wander off into the dusty neighborhood. When I finally get back, 2:30 a.m., and curl into sleep on the floor of the guesthouse because the bed seems too soft a thing, surely some part of me—even beyond the part of me who's just drunk and self-pitying—wishes that my absence had been noticed.

In the light of morning, I'll be perched on an outside wall checking my e-mail via the neighbor's wireless connection, and I will receive a strange missive from my stepfather. "I love you and am so proud of you," he will write. And later, "I wish to die now." My stepfather is not a young man. He is nearly ninety. "I am so weak," he will write.

Still, I feel unprepared. My throat constricts.

"May God bless Dr. Kevorkian," he will write.

By the time I read the e-mail, my stepfather will have taken—or been given—a lethal dose.

My mother will be the one who is with him.

But I can't tell you that part.

I can't tell you because my mother won't tell me. Or she will, and I will not ask for clarifying details. And so I will not be sure of what happened.

When I wrote and published my teenage memoir, *Atlas of the Human Heart*, about the year I dropped out of high school and the years spent tripping through Asia and Europe broke and starry-eyed, my mother nearly disowned me.

She hardly appears in the book, but she read each inky page as betrayal.

I'd been so excited to show her that book. My favorite book. I'd finally told this story, this truth—or some attempt at it. I'd imagined my mother would be proud of me, would call it poetry, would think I was brave.

"You made me throw up," is what she said. "How could you do this to me?" And "I feel like Job." Job from the Bible.

I didn't say anything, and I'm a little rusty on my Bible references, but I understood that if she was Job, that made me the Devil.

"How could you do this to your *daughter?*" she demanded. "How is this supposed to make *her* feel?"

That's when I understood that I had written no poetry.

I had written something shameful.

I had been so excited about that publication day, that book tour. I'd sent out review copies and e-mailed magazine editors.

Now I hoped that not so many people would read it.

Maybe my stepfather would have liked the story better than my mother did, would have been proud of me, would have called it poetry, would have thought I was brave. But my stepfather did not read that book. My mother told him not to. And now my stepfather was dead, or he was dying, and how would I ever tell *this* story? I certainly wouldn't want to implicate my mother. I wouldn't want to say anything that I didn't know for sure. I certainly wouldn't want to ask.

The details might be a part of my story, but it is not my story alone. Still, how am I to convey my naked and human heart/soul—or even some small part of how I felt when my stepfather died—if I cannot tell you the specifics?

"In my experience, communication between the living and the dead has not been adequate," my stepfather has written in his e-mail. "I would like to foster that communication."

But my stepfather is not dead.

My mother is on the phone from their home in southern Mexico.

My girlfriend and I are already in the car, driving north.

"He's in a coma," my mother tells me. "The doctor was here. He's going to live. He didn't take enough of whatever he . . . He's just . . ." And the phone cuts out.

Through all that desolate northern New Mexico landscape, listening to Lucinda Williams and Johnny Cash, through those weird brown Utah mountains and canyons, too hot in the car and not enough bottled water, my cell phone rings and cuts out, my stepfather has not regained consciousness, my daughter has not received the money, my sister is praying, is chanting, my girlfriend will not apologize, does not know what I'm talking about. "What song?" she scowls. "I can't believe you think there was anything significant about that song. Can't people *sing*? Or is that not all right with you? You've always been so jealous."

I put quote marks around those words, but I'm not sure those are the exact words my girlfriend used. I cannot remember. Dialogue is one of the things one must recreate in memoir. "You're allowed to recreate the dialogue," I tell my students. "It's understood that you weren't carrying a tape recorder."

Maybe I will show this story to my girlfriend later and ask her if she remembers it any differently. Maybe I won't. Suffice it to say that nearly two years later, those are the words that have carved themselves into my memory.

Maybe we didn't even talk about the song.

Maybe we were listening to Steely Dan.

My stepfather is dying. Rock of a stepfather. High Sierra guide. Dignified priest. And I am consumed by fleeting arguments about a drunken song, sick with heartbreak, teeth clenched in humiliation, mind reeling with blame, preoccupied with a sixteen-year-old daughter who is in New York without an ATM card.

My stepfather is dying and I am hung over and feeling sorry for myself.

Maybe I don't need to tell this story after all.

Maybe my own authenticity isn't so important.

Still, I write it. I keep writing it. I write it because I want to convey something to you, and it's something that seems important. I write it because I want to tell you that if your life and your grief feel messy and shameful sometimes, too, that maybe it's not just you—you're like me, and we're everybody.

This is what it feels like to be human.

I write it because I want to apologize to my stepfather for being a drunk and unpoetic child.

I write it because . . . Well, I don't know why.

The truth, it turns out, doesn't really set you free.

The truth is kind of embarrassing.

The truth makes a lot of people call you and tell you to shut up, call you and tell you it isn't true, call you and tell you your memory is off, call you and tell you that you made them throw up, call you and beg, *How could you?*

As we roll into Idaho, my girlfriend asks me to read to her out of a borrowed Thich Nhat Hanh book about anger.

"I'm angry all the time and I don't know why," my girlfriend says.

Or maybe she doesn't say that. Maybe that's what Sandra Bullock says in that movie *Crash*. Anyway, my girlfriend says something like that. Or maybe she doesn't say anything and I imagine that's what she's thinking.

Idaho, Idaho. We pass a ranch that belongs to my grandmother's best friend, and when I see a Cadillac parked on the street I'm suddenly excited—my grandmother's best friend might be here—I *so* want to stop in and say hello. But my grandmother's best friend is rich and conservative and has beautiful manners and we are dirty and gay and we've been driving for fifteen hours and we wear tank tops that show our tattoos.

My grandmother's best friend is not a young woman. She is nearly ninety years old, and there's no telling if or when I will ever see her again.

Still, I don't ask my girlfriend to stop.

I keep reading the Buddhist book.

As we cross the border, finally, out of Idaho, my cell phone beeps back into range and there are several voicemail messages waiting. We pull over onto the side of the highway.

My daughter got the money wire. *Thanks.*

My mother has called a priest to do last rites.

My sister cries and smokes, calls upon the spirits who will ferry our stepfather over.

As his limbs go cold, my mother summons the *brujas* to wash his body.

My daughter wants to know what's going on.

Me, I'm hungover on the side of the highway like some bad, bad country song.

It's difficult even for the doctors to tell if my stepfather has died or not. A light radiates from his body. The area around his heart is still hot. But he is not breathing, has not been breathing for a long time. The area around his heart is still hot even as they take his body away to prepare him for cremation.

On the last night of *The Traveling Death and Resurrection Show*, after my final reading and performance, my Catholic priest stepfather lay down and died.

Maybe that's all I should have told you. Maybe I should take the rest back.

2

The Right
to Speak

What the Little Old Ladies Feel

How I Told My Mother about My Memoir

ALISON BECHDEL

I knew I would have to tell my mother that I was writing a memoir about my father. But I didn't do it until I'd been working on the book *Fun Home* for a year. I wanted to make sure I had enough of a purchase on the material so that no matter what kind of reaction she had, I wouldn't lose my grasp.

I decided to tell her in person, when I went to visit for Christmas. I was quite anxious about how to broach the topic, and on the nine-hour drive to her house, I rehearsed what I would say. I pretty much had my lines nailed down by the time I hit Scranton, not far from where she lives. The driving on this particular stretch of I-81 is always hairy, and all of a sudden a truck pulled into my lane just in front of me—I must have been in his blind spot. I had to swerve onto the median so I didn't get clipped.

I was pissed off. After I recovered, I sped up to the truck to get its license number. That's when I saw the logo on the side: It was a Stroehmann's Sunbeam Bread truck. My father had died after being hit by—and probably intentionally jumping in front of—a Stroehmann's Sunbeam Bread truck.

After that synchronistic little brush with death, the prospect of telling my mom about the book loomed rather smaller. And indeed, she took the news quite well. She didn't quite understand why I wanted-ed to reveal all our sordid family secrets to the general public, but she never tried to talk me out of it.

I know I hurt her by writing this book. She made that clear, but she also let me know that she grasped the complexity of the situation. At one point after *Fun Home* came out, she sent me a review from a local newspaper. It cited the William Faulkner quote: "The writer's only responsibility is to his art. . . . If a writer has to rob his mother, he will not hesitate; the 'Ode on a Grecian Urn' is worth any number of old ladies." Then the reviewer went on to say, "Rarely are the old ladies asked how they felt about it." Mom liked that—that someone was considering her side of the story.

I do feel that I robbed my mother in writing this book. I thought I had her tacit permission to tell the story, but in fact I never asked for it, and she never gave it to me. Now I know that no matter how responsible you try to be in writing about another person, there's something inherently hostile in the act. You're violating their subjectivity. I thought I could write about my family without hurting anyone, but I was wrong. I probably will do it again. And that's just an uncomfortable fact about myself that I have to live with.

Truths We Could Live With

ROBIN HEMLEY

Although my mother, Elaine Gottlieb, was a writer and wrote occasionally about me, she never wanted me to write about her. Until she told me so, I never imagined the possibility that she would forbid me. She was a short story writer and sometime novelist who, in her youth, had been one of the most promising writers of her generation, appearing in *The Best American Short Stories: 1946,* and counting among her ardent supporters John Crowe Ransom of *The Kenyon Review.* But her career waned over time: marriage to my father, his press, their translations of Isaac Bashevis Singer's work, my brother, my sister, me—we all chipped away at her time and energy and eventually her promise.

I grew up as a character in my mother's short stories—I even suggested one story to her. When I was eleven, I dreamed of a lizard doing yoga and told my mother she should write a story about it. She did, in her own fashion. She wrote a story about an eleven-year-old boy who, among other things, imagines a lizard doing yoga. The story, "The Lizard" was dedicated to me, published in *The Southern Review* and reprinted in *The O. Henry Prize* collection.

We were allies then.

Still, I felt uncomfortable when I'd occasionally read a short story in which a thinly veiled me was one of the characters and I'd read about some awful trait of mine that my mother had taken note of. A kind of literary scolding. There were many. When I complained, she'd say, "Honey, it's fiction. No one's going to know it's you." But of course, that itself was the fiction. I knew it was me and knew that my mother was recording for posterity my more unpleasant traits.

When I started writing stories of my own, my mother was fine with that. Oh, she had twinges of jealousy, but they were overridden by pride. Her own stories were published less and less frequently as literary tastes inevitably changed and she could no longer be described as "promising." But we continued to support one another, and I helped her publish her last short story, a beautiful piece called "The Dance at the End of the War," about her time at Black Mountain College studying with painter Robert Motherwell.

All was fine until I decided to write a memoir about my older sister Nola, a diagnosed schizophrenic who had died of a prescription drug overdose at the age of twenty-five, when I was fifteen. My mother was horrified that I wanted to write about our family as nonfiction. "Why can't you fictionalize it?" she asked. Funny, but what she considered fiction was closer to memoir with the names simply changed. I didn't want to change the names.

The tension this caused I simply incorporated into the book about my sister, *Nola: A Memoir of Faith, Art, and Madness*, which was in some ways less about my sister than about this very topic: what we have permission to write about and what we don't. As I come from a family of writers, I decided to use the various texts my family produced to triangulate the truth of my sister and my family's life. I brought in an autobiography my sister wrote in the last year of her life, some court documents, a short story by my mother that was essentially a story *à clef* (to coin a term) about my sister and myself, and a short story I wrote about the night before my sister died. This story had appeared in my debut story collection. My goal was to show that fiction or nonfiction didn't matter—the pain contained in either could be equally visceral and real. When my mother complained on the phone that she would have to become a hermit after I completed my book, I would go to my study and record the conversation nearly verbatim. I suppose there was an inherent brattiness in such a move, but I felt it was justified, even crucial.

My mother disagreed.

With her psychically looking over my shoulder as I wrote, I nonetheless wrote without showing her a word. I hardly showed it to anyone. I knew that I needed to write it to myself first and then I could let it out into the world. I struck a deal with her. I told her that I would show her the book after it was completed and that she could give me her suggestions and criticisms, which I would consider the way I'd consider the suggestions of an editor.

And so, when I finally completed the book, I had to fulfill my promise, but it was not as easy as that. In the time between starting the book and completing it, my mother developed severe glaucoma and macular degeneration. In order to keep my word, I had to read her the book chapter by chapter. So every night for two weeks, I drove to her apartment and read to her. While I knew that she wouldn't be pleased by all of it—the stigma of mental illness, the keen pain she felt at the loss of her beloved daughter, and the revelation that my mother had not been married to my sister's father, another stigma in my mother's eyes—I gambled that her pride in me as a writer and her love for me would win out.

But there was one section early on that I did not want to read to her. My father had died of a massive heart attack, his first, at the age of fifty-one. I was seven and my brother was five years older, and we were bundled to a friend's house that night while my mother—in the company of my sister, Nola, and my mother's good friend, the poet Patricia Goedicke—drove the fifty miles from Athens, Ohio, to Columbus where my father was in the intensive care unit. Our family physician, Dr. Goldsmith, grimly told my mother in private that my father wouldn't last the night and that she shouldn't return to Athens. My mother didn't listen. She had a congenital hearing problem and wore hearing aids in both ears for much of her life. But this was an emotional inability to hear, not a physical one. When she returned to the waiting room, Patricia and Nola awaited the prognosis. "Cecil is going to be fine," my mother told them. "Dr. Goldsmith said we could go home and get some rest and come back tomorrow." They drove back to Athens together.

In the middle of the night, Patricia was awakened by a phone call. It was Dr. Goldsmith. "Where's Elaine?" he said. "Cecil is fading fast."

Patricia raced over to our house and rang the doorbell. There was no answer, and she rang again and again. She peeked in the large picture window at the front of the house and spied my mother sitting in a chair with a drink in her hand, lights ablaze, her hearing aids apparently turned off.

To me, there was no more emblematic story of the way my mother handled crisis and ugly truths. She fictionalized them, as we all do to a certain extent. She made them into truths she could live with.

When Patricia told me this story, I knew I had to use it, but I also knew that there would arrive for my mother and me a moment when we would have talk to one another about the past, frankly and openly, rather than fictionalize or bury it. This was that moment, when I faced my nearly blind, nearly deaf mother, the object of so many restorative operations that failed really to restore anything. I stopped reading.

I knew that I could skip right over that passage and she wouldn't notice. Doing this would spare her some pain. But I also knew it would break my promise. I knew that it would undermine what I wanted to get across—to myself and to her. I started reading again.

I remember a deep silence after I finished. She sat for a while and so did I, barely moving, the way we used to wait on my grandmother's porch in the flight path of JFK for a jet to pass overhead before we could be heard again over the roar. Finally, she spoke. "That's not what I remember."

I'm not sure how I responded. If I know myself—and that's sometimes debatable—I tried to assuage my guilt by directing it outward and showing compassion for her. I probably told her how understandable her reaction was. I'm sure that part of my reaction was self-serving, the plea of a somewhat spoiled child: *please* don't make me take it out. I say that part of my reaction was self-serving, but not all of it. I did feel tremendous sadness over this episode and for her suffering. I had been so young when my father died. When I was finally brought home from our friends' house afterward, my first sight was my mother sitting in that same chair in which Patricia had found her. But now she wasn't alone. She sat there red-faced and in a daze, people milling around her, murmuring but saying nothing directly to her. When she saw me, she reached out her arms, and I rushed upon her and burst into tears, burying myself in the cushioned chair and her arms, given over fully to the grief of seeing my mother so alone in this room full of people. There was nothing else to do or say then.

When my sister died eight years later, my mother asked if I would like to talk to someone about it, and if I had been older, I might have said, *Yes, I would like to talk to* you *about it.* But I didn't have the self-knowledge to make that request. I was making it now.

I had written a book to make the request apparent. With my mother, there was no other way. Books, after all, were the language of our family, the only way we made ourselves fully known to one another.

Writing the Black Family Home

FAITH ADIELE

As a memoirist, I am called to track down, research, and write about family members. As an African, I am wired to define family in the broadest, ever-widening sense—nuclear, extended, ancestral, clan, village, region, tribe/ethnicity, nation, continent, race, gender. As the female descendant of Finnish and Swedish villagers who immigrated to America then migrated west, the descendant of Nigerian villagers who stayed home and got colonized for their trouble, I am heir to family-group histories that have been at best underrepresented, at worst misrepresented. My job is to wield memoir as the corrective.

Before my birth, my white family pressured my mother to dispose of me, a mixed-race fetus. They couldn't have known that I would spring from the womb ready to exhume and engrave our various family groups onto history, but they sensed I was trouble.

BECOMING

After my narrow escape, I grew up in exile, separate from the clan. In rural America, Mummi, my Finnish grandmother, and I sat at table, baking and crafting, while she tallied family members lost. It was costly: the process of Immigrating and Migrating and Becoming. Costly becoming Amerikkalainen and middle class. I learned we should remember family pioneers, all of them, though the ones who didn't survive the Becoming didn't get ink. Their names were whispered, not inscribed in family albums, their pictures few. I didn't yet know that my own un-photographed birth was one such whisper, that Mummi as she prepped me was herself caught between two erasures—her father declared dead and disappeared to a mental institution for forty years, her daughter declared wed but disappeared to a home for unwed mothers, secret for forty years as well.

Across the ocean, the father I'd never met had adopted the opposite strategy: silence. His reticence began in the late 1960s, during the bloody pogroms against our tribe. In the last letter we received before Nigeria descended into civil war, when I was three, he included rare family detail:

> I find it extremely uncomfortable to narrate my story regarding the mass killing of Easterners in Northern Nigeria. The Northerners just liquidated all Easterners living in the North and of course I lost a score of relatives there. . . .
>
> You remember that I used to have eight sisters and one brother. Two of my sisters plus my mother plus my father are all dead.

After four years of silence, we thought he too was dead. But finally, in the summer of 1971, he resurfaced. After writing several detailed letters about the war that we never received, he conceded to the nation-state, declaring his intention to start forgetting:

> [M]y monthly pay can hardly sustain the large dependents I have acquired as a result of the civil war (orphans, cripples and all sorts) all for a week! . . . The degree of damage and devastation is so great and so overwhelming that whatever is being done is only a drop in a limitless ocean! . . . We lost quite a number of dear ones to air-raids, bullets and shelling! Tunde died. Mercy died . . . Quite a number of our "clan" passed away and it is quite a torture to remember them and I would rather let the sleeping dogs lie (if I can help it). I find it quite unbearable at times to have to recall the tragedies we had to pass through and I wouldn't be doing Faith any good sending a catalogue of dead relatives! When she is older it will become part of the history she will have to piece together, I suppose.

Unbearable to have to recall. Nonetheless, I took his charge to history seriously. At age twenty-six, I got on a plane to Nigeria, pockets stuffed with copies of his letters and little else.

Nine months later, I, my mother's only child, was now the eldest of my father's four. Long the sole black member of my Nordic American family, I was now the sole white member of my Nigerian family. But stranger than the sudden accumulation of family were the politics of an African one. This family ran on roles and group goals, not personalities and individual desire. I was Becoming . . . a Member. Member of the powerful eldest daughters association, member of a clan that regulated our family unit, member of a tribe still seething within the tenuous nation-state, member of a nation still recovering from colonial rule. Member of the largest black family in the world: Nigerians, comprising one out of every five blacks on the Continent. One out of every ten blacks on the globe.

WALKING WITH METAPHOR

According to the belief system of the Igbo, my father's tribe, a human being is only half the person; the other half, the spirit-double, walks the spirit realm, determining one's fate. Shortly after finding and falling in love with my father and siblings in Nigeria, and my cousins in Finland and at random book signings in the United States, and my ancestors on ship manifests and institutional intake forms, I began to view them differently. They spoke to me the way the narrator in my memoirs did—a character on the page, an actor upon and recipient of history. We were Nordic servants and entrepreneurs, union organizers turned middle class, civil rights pioneers and first-generation college graduates, troubled men abandoning single mothers, African freedom fighters and fledgling feminists. All heroic, all flawed. Metaphors marched with me.

At times it occurs to me that I am exposing a person breathing within the metaphor. I'm like David Sedaris in his essay "Repeat after Me": "In my mind, I'm like a friendly junkman building things from the little pieces of scrap I find here and there, but my family's started seeing things differently. Their personal lives are the so-called pieces of scrap I so casually pick up, and they're sick of it. More and more often their stories begin with the line, 'You have to swear you will never repeat this.' I always promise, but it's generally understood that my word is no better than Henry's."

Henry is his sister Lisa's parrot, whom she's taught to repeat self-help affirmations. In the essay, Sedaris is visiting Lisa, who's in crisis. His news doesn't help: one of his books has been optioned; there might now be a film about their lives. They watch a movie that eerily mirrors their own family, and shaken, on the ride home, Lisa confesses to hitting (but not killing) an animal and then trying (rather comically) to murder it. As Sedaris starts to laugh, his sister puts her head on the steering wheel and starts to sob. He knows he should comfort her; instead, Sedaris admits, *I instinctively reached for the notebook I keep in my pocket.* The tragicomedy escalates when Lisa grabs his hand. *"If you ever," she said, "ever repeat that story, I will never talk to you again . . ."*

I rewind the live audio recording, and the irony of Sedaris repeating the line to an audience hooting with laughter invokes the brilliant opening line to *The Woman Warrior*, my first memoir model: *"You must not tell anyone," my mother said, "what I am about to tell you."* As both Sedaris and Maxine Hong Kingston knew, the story that follows these admonitions is so important—Lisa, as Sedaris describes her, so "kind and just," Kingston's aunt so wronged by patriarchy—that it's clear we *need* to hear their struggles. For Kingston, exhuming a peasant-aunt-turned-ghost, claiming narrative history seems a moral imperative.

Sedaris, for his part, has the decency to imagine the movie-version ending of the story, wherein a Sedaris-like character sneaks down to the kitchen at night to teach his sister's parrot to say, *"Forgive me, forgive me, forgive me."*

FORGIVE ME

I warn student writers of the hazards of writing family. I tell them about the undergraduate who penned a charming child's account of growing up with an alcoholic mother. Her classmates so sympathized with the seven-year-old narrator eyeing her mother's breakfast oj and praying, *No vodka*, that the author burst into tears, terrified she'd frozen her beloved (and long since recovered) mother in infamy. Students chuckle at her reaction to success on the page, and I give the happy-ending postscript that the girl shared the story with her mother, who was stunned at the child's awareness and anxiety. Each apologized; their relationship deepened.

Then I tell them about a graduate school friend who wrote a luminous, generous piece exploring gender in her family. One image describes carefree beach holidays with her father, where she would build him a sandcastle table for his highball. When the essay was published, her father accused her of publicly portraying him—in that one sunny sentence—as an alcoholic. He stopped speaking to her. Students' mouths drop. Is the moral of the story, then, to write about alcoholic moms, but not social-drinker dads?

Here's the deal, I explain. Most people don't understand how memoir works, that it's one version of a truth, from a certain perspective, at a discrete moment in time. And your family, well, they'll *never* understand. How could they? If you can't agree on an account of what happened last Thanksgiving, how could you ever agree on a version of your entire childhood? There are precautions you can take, concessions you can make, but ultimately you've demonstrated a power your family doesn't have. Be prepared to lose them.

SUICIDE OR MURDER?

For my advanced courses on memoir, I've designed a unit named for Patricia Hampl's "Telling Other People's Secrets," an essay that begins, "Nighttime, and I have come here to sit alone in the dark . . . to tally up, finally, those I have betrayed. Let me count the ways." What she refers to as her "career of betrayal" began with a poem about her mother's epilepsy. "Let's start with mother, then, first betrayal." Like mine, Hampl's mother shaped her life around a secret that was passé by the time her daughter started writing. Nonetheless, Hampl's mother was outraged at what she considered her daughter's betrayal; Hampl, for her part, was outraged at what she considered her mother's melodrama: "I hadn't betrayed my mother—I had saved her. I freed her from silence, from secrecy, from the benighted attitudes that had caused her such anguish, and from the historical suppression of women's voices—and so on and so forth."

In a 1993 interview in *Poets & Writers* magazine, so-called confessional poet Sharon Olds also names it betrayal but says it's inevitable that *someone* is going to die *some* sort of death, no matter what a writer does:

> This is part of what I have come to think of as the spectrum of loyalty and betrayal. On the loyalty side is silence, . . . the poems not written, the thoughts not even thought, a kind of spiritual suicide of the writer and, perhaps, therefore, in a way, of a part of the culture. On the other side of the spectrum is song, and . . . perhaps very little consideration for other people's privacy, . . . a kind of destructiveness or spiritual murder. The way we learn our place on the spectrum seems to be the usual way of learning—by making mistakes.

So let's start making mistakes. I tell my students, Write the story you should not tell, the story that moves into the territory of other people's secrets, the story you feel may be worth risking relationship in service of your greater artistic mission. I give them their first line, Kingston's "You must not tell anyone . . . ," or Richard Rodriguez's similar confession in *Hunger of Memory*, "I am writing about those very things my mother has asked me not to reveal," or Hampl's ambivalent "[W]riters get to do this—tell secrets and get away with it. It's called, in book reviews and graduate seminars, courage."

I then ask them to consider their motives for breaking silence. It may be, like Hampl, to free family from the tyranny of outdated shames. It may be, like Kingston and Rodriguez, that their personal stories are regrettably intertwined with those of family members who don't want to reveal or examine their lives in the way the authors need to. It may be purely artistic—it's a great story, period. So what can be gained by revelation? Which stories are critical to us as artists, to the larger world?

The final part of the assignment is to rewrite or comment on the story in the voice of the person who didn't want it told. Use your creative powers, I urge them, to imagine yourself into that person's point of view. How have culture, personality, culpability, old shames shaped her stance? Can she understand what motivates you, the author? Have the two voices interact—a dialogue, letters, two versions separated by the safety of white space. I hope this final act of Imagining and Becoming won't silence but rather will prepare them. Hampl has a drawer stuffed with real letters from those who've cut her off: "I've lost quite a few people along the way. And not to death. I lose them to writing."

As the descendant of villagers, I know that the griot, the storyteller, is often the outcast, the crazy, but sometimes it's hard to know if we even qualify to be the village crazy, if we're equipped to heft the mad burden of silence-breaking. We can pray our motives are pure, but is that enough? If, as I believe, art requires risk on the part of its maker, does the answer lie in having something at stake ourselves, in knowing what we are willing to risk?

LET ME COUNT THE WAYS

I think I'm willing to risk nearly everything. Like the young Hampl, I'm arrogant; I too feel "heroic in a low-grade literary sort of way. I understood that my poetry—my poem!—had performed this liberating deed. My mother had been unable to speak. I had spoken for her. It had been hard for both of us. But this was the whole point of literature, its deepest good, this voicing of the unspoken, the forbidden. And look at the prize we won with our struggle." And though she's self-mocking, Hampl is correct. There is a prize. To be able to create family members as full, believable characters requires great empathy and imagination. We must separate ourselves from relationships and recognize our relatives as human, in weakness and strength. It was through researching sociohistorical context and birthing my parents on the page that I was finally able to understand the volatile temper of the young white mother who raised me alone, the decisions of the idealistic black father who left America without ever having seen me and chose postcolonial Africa over me. Again and again.

And if the mail I receive from imprisoned men and half-African kids in small-town USA is any indication, when I forgave my parents, a generation of unfathered black men and multiracial New World Africans moved closer to forgiving their fathers and mothers too. On the spectrum, certainly that broader family deserves some of my loyalty as well.

SURPRISING COSTS

Ironically, despite his 1971 charge to recover history, my father forbade me to write about him. "Wait until I'm gone," he would declare airily, "then you can write what you want." I would grit my teeth and smile; after all, he lived on another continent, and my only allegiance was to my mother. *Her* sole complaint was that I tended to romanticize her. But when my father died four years ago, I discovered that I *had* felt constrained to respect his name, had in fact blocked from memory entire events—though to protect him or myself is not clear. I do worry about my siblings' reactions to what I write about him. There's no longer any such thing as another continent; when I was living in Pennsylvania and a New York magazine published an essay about my meeting my siblings, my brother read it in Nigeria before I received my copy.

As a memoirist, at times I'm still surprised at the cost. While the ink was still drying on the contract to do the documentary about me, the director and producer pounced: "So, when do we fly to your mother's?" My mouth dropped as my heart sank. The evening the film aired, all of my mother's closest friends, along with the American viewing public, learned that she was actually unmarried and had birthed me in a home. Of course it was 2004, not 1963, and she had long since retired from teaching, so no one gave a damn. But still, it had been her secret for four decades. Hers. We'd quarreled about it exactly once. At lunch with a mutual friend, I'd refused to give the usual stock answers about my parentage.

Mom took me to task in the ladies' room: "It's *my* secret, and you forced me to reveal something I didn't choose to reveal to this friend, at this time."

"Well, it's my secret too," I'd countered, "and *I* don't want to keep it anymore." Didn't my claim trump hers? It was my origin tale, after all! "I can't support the American mythology that all families are hetero, married, nuclear, mono-racial. If someone just *assumes*—'So, when did your parents divorce?'—I *have* to respond, 'Who ever said they married?'"

We stared at each other. Throbbing in the air between us was the knowledge that if our family had been able to speak openly in the first place, I wouldn't have been born in secret, raised on government cheese, working every day to reject labels like *bastard* and *Tragic Mulatta*. I consoled my guilty conscience with the knowledge that we all murder our parents eventually.

Then, years later, the night before shipping the final pass to PBS, the film editor called with a last-minute offer: she could omit the reference to the home for unwed mothers, the footage of my mother talking about being disowned if she didn't get an illegal abortion and contemplating suicide.

"Oh no," Mom said when I called to pass on the message. "I knew as soon as I agreed to help with your project that this day would come. What's the point in telling half a truth?"

UNBEARABLE RECALL

When writer Amy Hempel asked Sharon Olds about her "famous Spectrum of Loyalty and Betrayal," for *BOMB* magazine, Olds explained that "each writer has to decide [where song begins and ends] over and over." As an African, I feel the same dilemma writing about blacks (my global family) as I do my (nuclear) family. My hardest piece so far was an essay on legacies of violence in Nigeria. It started with those on top—colonial powers and neocolonial global lenders and military dictators all exploiting citizens; moved to those at bottom—unpaid soldiers beating university students, the downstairs neighbors beating their housegirl; and ended at home—my host father beating my host mother. I sobbed as I wrote it, from both the pain of the past remembered and the fear of the future awaiting its publication. Would I compound the insidious misinformation about Deepest, Darkest Africa? About the black family? Would I break the heart of the Nigerian family that sheltered me during the months my (blood) father rejected me? Would my words do harm?

I revised for years. I wove in historical context. I forced myself to love every character—the bruised housegirl, my stressed host parents, even the hungry soldiers. In the end, I included myself, slapping a child, in the chain of violence and sent it to an African journal to decide its fate. They published it beautifully, adding black-and-white images by a Nigerian photographer. An award-winning writer known for her work on morality and faith said it was the single best piece about culture shock she'd ever read. I felt gratified. I felt relieved. And every time I read the essay, I cry, wondering whom I've betrayed.

The Deeper End of the Quarry

Fiction, Nonfiction, and the Family Dilemma

DINTY W. MOORE

The first time that I wrote honestly about family secrets was in a short story documenting my mother's weakness around alcohol, including a particular time when she had fallen spectacularly off the wagon. My mom was in her late sixties at the time that she had this episode, and I wrote the story about six months later. The story covered the events of my sister discovering the drinking, then calling me on the phone, and our various attempts at intervention.

I remember pulling actual phone conversations out of real life and inserting them into the early drafts. Other details about my mother's hidden habit—including some of the dialogue between mother and son—were also notably close to what had really occurred. Though I identified primarily as a fiction writer back in those days, had not yet made the turn in my career to creative nonfiction, there was an undeniable element of memoir in that short story.

But this *was* fiction, so I changed my own name to James, gave my sister a new name (Loretta), and moved everything a hundred or so miles south of where I was raised to a similar but different small industrial town.

The most dramatic change I made was to add an epiphany at the end, a culminating moment that bore no resemblance to the truth, but had a poetic sense of closure. The protagonist, the thinly veiled version of me, at wit's end about his complicated family drama, dives into an abandoned quarry, now filled with water, and attempts to remember life in the womb:

I stay deep in the water, warm and wet, and try to imagine just exactly how it was for me, before birth, when this was all I knew. I try to remember what I was thinking, three decades back, when I was still inside of Marge.

And as I slowly rise, my air depleting, as I float back to the water's mirrored surface, I remember something. Small memories from a time before memories are supposedly possible. Thought without language.

I remember, of course, being very small and very crowded. But the other thing I remember, the thing that surprises me, is that I was most of all curious. I remember that I really couldn't wait to see how things turned out.

A moment later I come up for air, trying to hold that feeling.

All of these years later, that ending seems a bit melodramatic, but it worked well enough, and the story was picked up by an excellent literary journal. Titled "The Deep End," this story was, like much fiction, thinly veiled autobiography. If you knew me, knew my life and family, and you read that story in a magazine, your ears would perk up. *Boy,* you might think, *that all sounds awfully familiar.*

As it turns out, the sister in question (actually, I have two sisters, but for the sake of fictional compression, there was only one in the story) did run across "The Deep End" in the literary journal, and she was touched, even by an unflattering detail I had lifted from her own life and given to her doppelganger character. ("I didn't realize you understood me so well," was her reaction to this undeniably uncomfortable element.)

So, that was good, but then my sister (Susan, in real life), decided to show this story to our mother.

I never quite understood why, or what she intended, and I wasn't there when my mother read the words I had written, but Susan phoned me later that day with a full report.

"You know that story of yours? I showed it to Mom."

Stunned silence.

"Don't you want to know what she said?"

"Jesus, Susan."

"She sat there and read the whole story, page by page, and didn't utter a word. And then, when she was done, she put the magazine down on the table, looked up at me, and said, 'Oh that Dinty. How *does* he think this stuff up?'"

"She said what?"

"'How *does* he think this stuff up?'"

Susan laughed at that point, and I did too. We were sharing a bit of sibling humor, acknowledging our mom's stubbornness and resilience. Throughout her life, if a fact or situation was inconvenient, she would pretend it wasn't there. And she could pretend very convincingly.

I don't, of course, know what my mother really thought of the story, if she even recognized herself and her children, or if the human capacity for denial had simply made it easier for her to see the fictionalized world that I had created while the reality of the tale drifted dimly into the background.

That was the last she ever spoke of my story, and to be honest, I was relieved.

I did, as I've mentioned, eventually make the move to creative nonfiction as my primary genre. I began to write honestly about my father's struggles with alcoholism, but he had passed away at this point. By the time I was willing to publish nonfiction accounts of my mother's struggles with depression, painkillers, drinking, and more importantly, the residue of her own tragic childhood in her adult life and the lives of her children, she had passed on as well.

Both of my sisters have by and large been supportive of me in this endeavor. One of my first cousins, I have heard by secondhand report, is not so supportive and tells others among the cousins that I should lay off the family secrets and cease being disloyal to my father and mother.

But the fallout has been mild, to say the least. And let me say here that I truly love and honor both of my parents, despite the imperfections and mistakes. What I believe is that the straightforward telling of family stories has value. I believe that more people have been harmed over time by secrets and concealment than by candor and revelation.

But then I tripped myself up.

Ten years ago I attempted what I thought would be my third book of nonfiction, a look at fathers and daughters, an autobiographical account of my relationship with my smart, sassy pre-teen, and an attempt to wrestle with the issues raised by Mary Pipher in her important *Reviving Ophelia: Saving the Selves of Adolescent Girls*, a book that examines what Pipher calls our "girl-poisoning culture."

When I would tell people about this book, or read excerpts, or mention my concerns for my own daughter, I received universally positive reactions. "That's important, Dinty. Write it," folks would say at conferences. Even now, ten years later, people still ask me, "Whatever happened to that book?"

Well, despite a nifty advance, the interest of two publishers, and the support of two excellent editors, the book eluded me, kept ringing false, wouldn't resolve itself in any satisfying way.

I estimate that I wrote upwards of 1,200 pages of material to complete the first "finished" draft of that book. I'm a constant reviser, so when I say "finished" draft, I'm talking twenty to thirty drafts at a minimum of each chapter. And yet, it wasn't working, refused to take successful shape. The first publisher eventually lost interest.

Stubborn (like my mother, perhaps), I embarked on a second attempt, a radical rethinking and reshaping of the book, and produced heaven only knows how many fresh pages, while entirely retooling what I recycled from the first iteration. A second publisher came on board.

All in all, this project consumed five years. And the book has still not seen the light of day.

One July afternoon, I sat in my agent's office, having driven into Manhattan just for the day, so we could discuss the next step with my stalled project. "Why don't you set it aside?" she suggested after some mutual hand wringing. "Give the book a rest, and who knows, may- be you will come back to it in a few years. Let's see what else you have to work on."

I wanted to throttle my agent right then and there, and might have if I were not a believer in nonviolence (or if the receptionist had not been in such close hearing range). After all of this work, sweat, ago- ny, she wanted me to set it aside, just like that?

I sputtered, she patted me down with consoling words, I sputtered some more, and left her office in a state of suppressed rage, shock, despondency, and confusion.

Thirty minutes later, though, as I headed home across the George Washington Bridge, I felt as if the proverbial load had been lifted from my shoulders. My agent was right. Despite the hard work, the sound- ness of my initial idea, the moments in the book that worked quite well (but not well enough to make the book complete or coherent), the project was making me unhappy, was likely to remain stalled for years to come, and my stubbornness to "finish what I had started" was sucking the life from my writing practice.

Now, that book is dead, abandoned forever, and what I have sal- vaged is an eight-page essay that pretty much summarizes everything I was trying to say, in a fairly comic manner.

People tell me it is a good essay.

And after five years of work, it should be.

So what happened? Why did this particular project pose a storytell- ing problem that I could never bring myself to solve?

I came to conclude that I failed because I was not and could not be fully honest in the writing of the book. I found myself caught be- tween two competing loyalties—loyalty to my writing and loyalty to my daughter—and this dishonesty, the careful tiptoeing around to avoid this or that little truth, doomed my project from the start.

It is the writer's duty, I believe, to view the world with no filters over the eyes, no rose-colored glasses distorting what is really seen, no glossing over the truth for the sake of politeness or propriety. Let the scales fall away.

It is the duty of parents, on the other hand, to look at their children and *not* see the possible faults, *not* concede the probable weaknesses. A parent, to my mind, is fully obligated to double-up on the rose-colored glasses and give the kid as much leeway and as generous an interpretation as possible. None of us is perfect, like it or not, but it is *not* the parent's job to be the bearer of that disappointing news.

My daughter is, and was, a brilliant, resourceful, delightful human being, but was she perfect? Well, yes and no. She was (and is) perfect because I love her that much, but she has struggled with some of the very issues Pipher outlines in her book, and my daughter—it is hard for me to even put this in print here, though I feel sure she would agree with me—has her own weaknesses, her blind spots, and her anxieties.

If I were to do justice to my topic, to the themes that are central to Pipher's message, and to the truth, the book I was attempting to finish would require me to be entirely forthcoming about my concerns and misgivings, and would require that I confess those moments where I was—let me just say it—making judgments and finding, or fearing, fault.

I have written of being the child of alcoholic, depressive parents, of how the shattered families that my parents survived had a direct impact on my own troubled childhood, but, of course, my daughter is just one short generational step away from that legacy. Do I have worries? Sure I do.

Did my daughter sense my concern, my misgivings, my doubts about her and about myself during her teenage years? Sure she did, more than a few times. But that's different from putting it all down on the page, discussing it without filter or censor, and making it public.

Other writers have negotiated this path, for good or for ill, but I could not. And all the clever side stepping in the world didn't mask this from the reader. When something, a book or a story, doesn't ring true, it doesn't ring true. That's part of the challenge of art, and part of the beauty as well.

The quarry of family secrets has a deep end, full of darkness and uncertainty, and writers who dive down into that material are going to have to learn to swim, and breathe underwater, while still holding their eyes wide open.

But that quarry has a deeper end still, at least in my experience, and I simply couldn't take it. I had to come up for air.

Mama's Voices

SUSAN OLDING

PLAY

When my daughter Maia was twenty-one months old, I left her for ten days to attend a writers' conference in Vermont. Maia stayed at home with my husband, who took some time off work. From the moment of her adoption at the age of ten months, Mark had been a full partner in caring for her. True, I prepared her bottles and cuddled her and played with her more often; I planned her days and spent more hours in her company. But if she woke with a cry in the night, Mark went to her as often as I did. As the father of three older children—by then, young adults—he knew how to change a diaper, when to sneak a tickle, where to look for the missing blankie, what to do for an owie, and whom to phone in an emergency. Yes, I was her mother. But her dad was the more experienced parent.

Also in the house with us all that spring and summer was one of Mark's older children, Noah. Early evenings, he'd perch on the steps of our west-facing front porch, a Corona in one hand and a book in the other. Maia followed him there, clad only in a diaper, her skin still damp and smelling of the baby oil we squirted in her bath. She plopped down beside him, grabbing his book with clumsy fingers and losing his place in the text, calling out to every dog that ambled past. Noah taught her how to blow across the beer bottle to produce a sound. From the kitchen where I stood preparing supper, I'd hear first his bass blast and then her fainter, eager echo.

Most weekdays while I was away, Maia spent several hours—my writing hours—with her regular babysitter, Sue, just as she would have if I had been home. At Sue's, the air smelled like flowers and lemon furniture polish. Sue wore denim overalls and a big silver cuff and silver necklaces and earrings, and on sticky afternoons, from the deep recesses of her freezer, she produced juice popsicles, translucent as jewels in the sun. Maia sucked on them and then rolled on the floor with the dogs or splashed in the cool water of the swimming pool, supervised all the while by the woman who, over the years, had cared for each of Mark's older children in their turn, and many other children besides.

None of that could make up for my absence. A toddler needs her mother. Everybody knows that. A toddler who has lived in an orphanage for most of her first year needs her mother even more. Afraid of how our separation might affect Maia, I planned for my departure with the diligence of a general preparing for battle. I read the experts, most of whom declared that she would manage fine, with support, and emerge from the experience stronger. I played countless games of hide and seek—*Mama goes away, Mama comes back*—and then we practiced—*one whole day apart, one night apart*—and I gauged her reaction on my return. I gave her a photo of the two of us, my high-beam smile turned on her, my arms protectively curved round her body. I searched the library for kids' stories about mothers who travel for work. I gave her an old red plaid shirt of mine and watched as she sniffed it and claimed it. And I gave her a basket of gifts—one for each night I'd be gone, a tangible calendar—each present wrapped in brightly colored tissue and all of them placed in a big basket. She still has some of those toys. A plastic tea set. A clock with hands that move, for teaching time. And the biggest gift, the most extravagant— a Little Tykes tape recorder.

Mark set up the machine that first night and turned it on. Maia watched, solemn and apprehensive, as the homemade recording crackled and hissed. Then she smiled. "Who's that?" Mark asked. "Mama!" she crowed, swaying back and forth in her excitement. "Mama's . . . *voices!*"

FAST FORWARD

Four years later, I am on my way to the famous writers' conference for a second time. The day of my flight, I meet with an agent in Toronto. He has read an essay of mine in a literary journal and wants to discuss it with me. He likes the piece—likes it a lot—and over coffee at an outdoor café, he asks whether I'd consider expanding it into a book. If I write that book, he would very much like to see it.

Light hits the green leaves of the vines growing up around the patio trellis. Light dances over the spoons, the knives, the porcelain cups. I sip my black Americano, savor its bitter brightness.

The encounter is an emerging writer's dream come true. Or, as my instructor at the conference will put it, "The Schwab's Drug Store fantasy."

STOP

"The Schwab's Drug Store fantasy" *is* a fantasy. Lana Turner, said to have bewitched a talent scout with her beauty while sipping a cola at the soda counter there, was actually discovered at the Top Hat Café. The Top Hat sits across the street from Hollywood High School, where Lana, then known as Judy, was an indifferent student. She may have been drinking a Coke, as the legend goes, but more likely she skipped out of class to sneak a cigarette.

PLAY

The tape I made for Maia included nursery rhymes—traditional favorites like Wee Willie Winkie and Banbury Cross and Baa Baa, Black Sheep, and modern-day versions by Eric Carle and Sandra Boynton. I recorded stories she already knew, like *Goodnight Moon* and *Runaway Bunny*, and stories that were new to her. Maia hadn't warmed to any of the commercially available books about adoption, so I wrote and read onto tape a version of her own story, explaining how she came to be our daughter. I told anecdotes about my childhood and about her grandparents, to strengthen her sense of history and connection to our family. I read Chinese legends, to strengthen her connection to the country and culture of her birth. I read Blake, and Coleridge, and Keats. I read Lear and Lewis Carroll. Words for counsel. Words for encouragement. Words for information and education. Words for the pure, sweet beauty of words.

FAST FORWARD

In the years between visits to the famous writers' conference, I have written little. Little for publication, that is. Instead, I've filled out dozens of doctors' forms, responded to psychologists' questionnaires, and recounted increasingly bleak descriptions of my life as a mother to parent support groups on the Internet. In the years between visits to this conference, my active, delightful toddler has disappeared and been replaced by a raging, resistant, impulsive changeling. Maia's violence has to be seen to be believed. She picks up chairs and throws them. She pokes her fingers into our eyes. She kicks. She bites. She scratches.

I have tried to understand. I have tried to find help and therapy. I have spent a small fortune on parenting books and have tried, fruitlessly, to follow their recommendations. I am getting used to the disdain or pity of strangers. I am getting used to feeling lonely. I've lost friendships over this; people think it's my fault, that I must be doing something wrong; people, understandably, get tired of my complaining.

The essay the agent likes is the story of our struggle. It is dark and ambiguous and does not offer answers, easy or otherwise.

STOP

Lana Turner described her life as "a series of emergencies." That's an understatement. The first emergency was the murder of her father. John "Virgil" Turner gambled at cards. Once, he boasted too loudly about the tricycle he planned to buy for his only daughter with his winnings. His killer took the money and Lana never got her bike. Instead, she and her mother moved to Los Angeles, where a decade later she began her career, eventually appearing in fifty-four movies, as well as performing in radio, on television, and for the theater. She became one of the highest-paid women in America. Yet for all her outward success, she never garnered much respect for her work, and at least once, depressed over a box-office flop, she attempted suicide. A lifelong alcoholic, she was married eight times to seven different husbands. One marriage was annulled and the rest ended in divorce. Her love affairs with famous men—Tyrone Power, Howard Hughes— were similarly unhappy and short-lived. Inherited Rh-factor complications ruled out the large family she had dreamed of, but she did bear one child, a daughter, who was only saved from death at birth by an immediate blood transfusion.

FAST FORWARD

Famous names, clever classmates, gold clapboard buildings, wine and cocktails on a wide veranda overlooking stubble fields and the rumpled shoulders of Robert Frost's fabled Green Mountains. This is the conference. Every morning, in a converted, whitewashed barn called the Little Theatre, over a hundred of us gather to hear faculty and fellows talk about the writing life. *Follow your obsessions*, they say. *Write about what matters to you. Write what bothers you, what you can't get your head around. Write what keeps you awake.* Later, in class, we critique one another's efforts and our instructors advise: *Bring authority of significance to your own stories.* Afternoons, we hike in the woods and pastures. New York agents and editors come to call. And every night, the moon ascends over the mountains and two hundred of us leave our rooms in the clapboard dorms and file into the Little Theatre again, and the screen doors swing shut and the lights go down—all except for one light at the podium, like a campfire glowing in darkness. We angle ourselves onto folding chairs, pull our sweaters tighter against the chill, and listen as one after another the authors take the stage, and above the trilling of crickets, above the din of our own minds, their voices rise—whispering, beseeching, correcting, caressing, complaining, explaining, shouting, persuading, teasing, berating, comforting, lying, and laying it on the line—a symphony of sound, resonating to the rafters, leaving enduring echoes, weaving indelible magic.

PLAY

Every morning, I called home. I woke early, still on toddler-time. Mist veiled the mountains. Dew dampened the hems of my jeans as I crossed the lawn to an old-fashioned phone booth that stood in the field next to the laundry compound. I dialed the number, waited for the ring.

"I love you, Sweet Bean."

"Mama. I went to the park. I throwed a ball. I swam in the pool."

"The pool! Was the water cold?"

"A tiny tiny *tiny* bit cold."

The sound of breathing. In the background, Mark walking past, heavy-heeled on our creaky wood floors. A cupboard door closing. Then, "Mama. Where are you?"

I drew faces on the booth's foggy glass. A smiley face. A puzzled face. A frown. "How's she doing?" I'd say to Mark when he came on the line.

"She's fine," he assured me. "She's happy. She loves the tapes."

STOP

If Lana Turner had hoped for an easy child, her daughter, Cheryl Crane, must have proved a disappointment. Spoiled and sullen-looking in her early photos, Cheryl later became rebellious and unruly. She had her reasons. At ten, she confided that her mother's current husband, Lex Barker, or "Tarzan," had been sexually abusing her for the past three years. To her credit—considering how desperate she was for male attention and approval—Lana defended her daughter. In a performance worthy of one of her films, she withdrew a gun from a drawer next to her sleeping husband's bed, nudged the muzzle to his ear, and said, "Get out."

Four years later, Cheryl assumed the role of avenging female. For some time, Lana had been trying to extricate herself from an abusive relationship with a small-time hoodlum named Johnny Stompanato. Stompanato refused to leave. One night Cheryl overheard them fighting in her mother's room and became frightened. As their voices rose in anger and Stompanato began threatening to cut her mother's face—the family's livelihood—and to hurt her grandmother, she ran to the kitchen and grabbed a carving knife, which happened to be lying on the counter. (Happened to be lying on the counter?) Returning upstairs, she begged her mother to open the door. Stompanato stood with his back to her, leaning over her mother, grasping something in his hands—a weapon, Cheryl believed, or so she later said, although in fact he held a bundle of his clothes, still clinging to their hangers. Over her mother's frantic protests, Cheryl lunged and stabbed him.

FAST FORWARD

One of my obligations as a scholar at this conference is to give a reading in the Little Theatre. I think about reading from the essay about my daughter and my stomach clenches. That piece is too long, too personal, too difficult to excerpt, too domestic, too dependent on all its parts for a true effect, I tell myself. What I mean is, that piece is too revealing, too raw. Or maybe it's just too real. I scroll through the documents folder on my laptop, looking for something more suitable.

But walking out by the river one afternoon, reflecting on the history of this place, counting the names of writers who've come here in the past—Anne Sexton, Truman Capote, Toni Morrison, May Sarton, Ralph Ellison—I am overcome by an ideal of literature as life-changing. *Write your obsessions, write what matters to you, write what you can't get your head around.* That's what those writers did. They wrote about sex and madness and death and childhood and loneliness and race and their stories came from their own lives and they didn't play it safe. I'm playing with the thought of a book. When else will I get to test this material on so large an audience? Suddenly, it seems cowardly not to read from this essay, the essay that I might—or might not—expand. After all, what's the worst that could happen? Nobody here knows me. Nobody knows my daughter.

I approach the podium, peer into the lights, pretend to look at an audience that I can't see through the glare. Leaning hard onto the surface of the wood to prevent myself from shaking, I read. And surprise—it's over almost before I know it. Afterward, I look up from my pages to find myself surrounded. Editors of journals press their cards into my hand, inviting submissions. Faculty members offer congratulations. Days later, participants collar me in the cafeteria line or sidle closer under the shade of those wide verandas. *My son was like that. My wife works with kids like yours. My cousin just adopted a kid like the one you wrote about. My sister-in-law has two daughters like that.* Everyone, it seems, has a similar story. Everyone wants to know more.

I try not to become too inflated with self-regard.

STOP

An exciting new voice. A bold, authentic voice. A stylish, urban voice. A raw, unvarnished voice. A mature voice in full possession of its powers. Loved the voice! Sorry, we didn't like the voice. I've found/lost my voice.

FAST FORWARD

With my instructor's permission, I substitute this piece for the one I'd originally submitted, and ask my classmates to consider how it might be expanded, opened up, for a book. I don't know what I expect. Probably more of what happened at the reading. Most of my classmates are working on books themselves. Some of my classmates were in that audience, some were part of the group that later surrounded me. So what happens comes as a rude surprise.

Here are the things my classmates say: *Hard to say how you could do this; you're still in the middle of it. It's not your story. It's your daughter's story. You shouldn't write this. It's too risky for your child. You'll ruin your daughter's life. Can't see this as a book. It's wrong to write about a child. Don't worry. You'll find other subjects. If you must write this, put it in a drawer.*

Here is what our Teaching Fellow says. (She's a girl; she wears ankle-strap wedges in dark red kid, the kind that Lana Turner might have worn, and I want a pair.) *Ethically, this is wrong. It would represent a huge betrayal. Writing it would violate confidentiality, and would irreparably damage your relationship with your daughter.*

Here is what my instructor, the famous memoirist, says: *Renunciation is also a part of the writing life. I would worry about you as a person and a writer if you pushed yourself into the limelight with this material. Save yourself as a writer.*

STOP

Lana Turner died in 1995 of throat cancer.

FAST FORWARD

My Canadian reserve collapses. Tears gush from my eyes, trail down my cheeks, and trickle to my chest. I think of Niagara Falls. More water on *our* side. My classmates pretend they don't notice. They keep on talking, saying again what they've already said. Nobody offers me a break. Nobody offers a tissue. I wipe my face with the back of my bare arm. The woman beside me, a therapist in her regular life, fishes in her bag and retrieves a thin paper napkin, the kind you find on the tabletops of diners in aluminum dispensers, the kind that Lana Turner might have dabbed to her lips when a stranger approached her in the Top Hat Café with his card. My classmate hands me this napkin before resuming her arguments against my project. Her eyes are soft and brown but something in their expression reminds me of a puppy you might find digging up your garden. He's sorry. But only because he's been caught.

At the midpoint of the workshop, after they are done with me and ready to move on to the next victim, I try to get into the bathroom. But someone has beat me to it, so I spend the next hour piggy-eyed, blotchy, and silent throughout discussion of my classmate's submission. My tears continue to flow. I have never cried this much in public. I can't remember the last time I cried this much, period. Maybe when I was my daughter's age? After class, my humiliation complete, I retreat to my room, where I lie facedown on the bed. Like the schoolgirl I've been reduced to.

STOP

The symptoms of cancer of the throat, or larynx, depend mainly on the size and location of the tumor. Most cancers of the larynx begin on the vocal cords. These tumors are seldom painful, but they almost always cause hoarseness or other changes in the voice.[1]

FAST FORWARD

I wear sunglasses to my meeting with the instructor. I apologize for crying in class.

"Oh," she says. "No need to apologize. We all come here for professional validation and advancement. I *expected* you to break down. I just wasn't sure when."

Behind my glasses, I blink, grateful for their protection.

"You know," she muses, "your story reminds me a bit of one that I have wanted to write for a long while, about a friend of mine who is a priest . . . and a pedophile. Nobody wants me to write this story. People don't want to hear that he might not be evil, or that I might want to know him anyway."

She's been wearing sunglasses, too. She takes them off. Her face, round, pale, and unlined, does not betray her age, does not reveal a thing about who she might be. "I haven't written that story," she says. "It makes people uncomfortable."

STOP

> *I've promised my family that each may pass on the book. I've promised to take out anything that anyone objects to—anything at all. . . . I don't believe in a writer's kicking around people who don't have access to a printing press. They can't defend themselves.*
>
> ANNIE DILLARD, *in "To Fashion a Text"*

> *Writers are always selling somebody out.*
>
> JOAN DIDION, *in* Slouching Towards Bethlehem

> *Writing . . . is like rearing children.*
>
> ANNIE DILLARD, *in "To Fashion a Text"*

1. MedicineNet, WebMD, San Clemente, California, July 8, 2011. www.medicinenet .com.

REWIND

Write about what obsesses you. Write what bothers you, what you can't get your head around. Write what keeps you awake.

My daughter is what obsesses me. My daughter keeps me awake.

RECORD

Once upon a time there was a writer who could spin words into gold. She was as gentle as she was gifted, and as kind as she was keen, and growing up, she paid close attention to her unusual and unhappy family and to her feelings about them—as most writers do. Her first book, a collection of pellucid autobiographical stories, won the acclaim of critics, the admiration of readers, and the agony and ire of the family members she had drawn upon in creating her "troubled" characters. The writer smiled modestly for the cameras and took her bows in public, winced and grieved and repented in private, and then, like all good writers, she sat down to work on Book Number Two. But before she got far into it, the writer married and bore children, and the children needed nursing and then their noses needed wiping and then they needed clothes and books and college funds, and the writer took a job, because Book Number Two wasn't finished yet and not even the strong sales of her first collection could feed her ravenous family.

Nighttimes, in her basement office, the writer wrote. But having used her family for the first book she was shy of doing so again. She worried that her work was too purely personal. She worried that she was nothing but a navel-gazer. She wanted to make a difference in the world. But between calls from the school and Halloween treats and dentist appointments and doctor appointments and nightly tuck-ins with her kids, the words came in fits and starts, jerky and then slow—so slow, so cryptic sometimes, that they felt almost like semaphore. So one day, on a tip from a good friend, the writer decided that she needed a change of genres. She would forget about writing stories for a while. She would take her gift for telegraphed images and write for television, write scripts that brought attention to serious political problems, scripts that showed she was more than a mere "domestic" scribbler, more than a navel-gazer.

Sure enough—because she was a good writer, a writer whose touch could turn anything to gold—success followed. Awards, articles in the press, offers of more work. The writer felt happy. She'd produced something that had reached a wide audience—a much wider audience than any literary book could reach. Something that might help others. Still—in the darkness of her basement office, her desk lamp beaming onto her brown hair, if she was honest with herself she had to admit it: she missed words. She missed language, her first love, and she longed to dive deep into a narrative. She was, after all, a writer.

One day, after a long dry spell, a story occurred to her. The story concerned a journey she had taken with her children. It touched on all her most pressing obsessions. Family *and* the world. Domestic *and* political. Not either/or. Both/and. Feverishly, she wrote up a proposal, thinking it through, checking it over, making sure it was the best that it could be. Then she printed it and left it on her desk for one last revision before sending it off to her agent. For the first time in many years, she felt excited and hopeful. This was her *real* material. She knew it.

That afternoon when she came home from work, her son—now on the verge of manhood—stood at her desk. His feet, a shoulder's width apart, seemed rooted to the floor. His face—that nose she'd wiped, those teeth she'd paid to straighten, those lips that had lisped his first words of love to her—was dark. He held the proposal in his hand. "Am I in this story?" he said.

The writer shivered, as at a sudden gust of wind. She watched the pages of her manuscript fly out of her son's hands and skirt the walls. Some of the pages sped out the window, scudded through the yard, and flapped against the trees and the telephone wires. Some of the pages soared up, up to the west, swooping and darting like seagulls until they disappeared in the wide dark. Some of those pages sped toward her open mouth, surged down her throat, gagged that scream that struggled to rise, wadded themselves into a lump, choked her.

"I don't want you to write about me," her son said.

The writer said nothing. There was nothing to say. She took the pages from her son and rent them to bits. Book Number Two did not appear.

STOP

Surgery to remove part or all of the larynx is a partial or total laryngectomy. In either operation, the surgeon performs a tracheostomy, creating an opening called a stoma in the front of the neck. (The stoma may be temporary or permanent). Air enters and leaves the trachea and lungs through this opening. A tracheostomy tube, also called a trach ("trake") tube, keeps the new airway open.

A partial laryngectomy preserves the voice. The surgeon removes only part of the voice box, just one vocal cord, part of a cord, or just the epiglottis, and the stoma is temporary. After a brief recovery period, the trach tube is removed, and the stoma closes up. The patient can then breathe and talk in the usual way. In some cases, however, the voice may be hoarse or weak.

In a total laryngectomy, the whole voice box is removed, and the stoma is permanent. The patient, called a laryngectomee, breathes through the stoma. A laryngectomee must learn to talk in a new way.[2]

FAST FORWARD

I do not talk much to my classmates outside of workshop. But one day one of them spies me in the lunch line. "I've been thinking," she says. "People *do* write about their kids. They write about them all the time. Maybe we were a bit hasty in class."

This is generous of her; if anyone has reason to feel threatened by the essay I wrote, she does. She was once a foster child. Her story, while not identical to my daughter's, echoes those themes of loss and longing and violence.

She's right, of course. People do write about their kids. But mostly they write print versions of those bare-bum-on-the-bear-rug photos. Gee willikers! What a little dickens! *Kids Say the Darnedest Things.* Their kids may hate them later, but more for lapses of taste than for any serious revelations about their lives.

2. MedicineNet.

STOP

Voice in writing, identified variously as style, persona, stance, or ethos, has never been very clearly defined, and, as a consequence, there has never been a consistent methodology for how to use it in the teaching of writing. Although these definitional and methodological problems have frequently been chronicled in the journals (see, for example, Hashimoto; Leggo), the voice metaphor, which emerged in the 1970s, remains extraordinarily popular . . . and has a strong presence in contemporary discussions of writing.[3]

REWIND

If you must write it, put it in a drawer.
    Put it in a drawer? Who am I, Emily Dickinson?
    Tell all the truth. But tell it slant.

FAST FORWARD

I meet on the grass with our Fellow. She of the pretty shoes, of the dire warnings and grave predictions. She, who looks so beautiful and so serious and so exhausted on the jacket photo of her first book, a memoir about her heroin-addict mother.

    I ask the question that's been bothering me. Was it something I said? Was there anything in that first essay—the one I brought to the class—was there anything in the *writing*, that led her to believe I might treat this material in an exploitative way?

    No, she says. It wasn't the writing. The writing was fine. But the situation was inherently exploitative. My daughter, I'd said, had been traumatized by her history of abandonment and orphanage neglect. To write a book about my daughter's trauma would be to reinscribe it. It would be a huge betrayal. "To a nonwriter, a book is the truth."

    "Suppose I wrote a book of poems?"

    "Oh." She pauses. "That would be okay. That would be different."

    But why?

---

3. Darsie Bowen, "The Rise of a Metaphor: 'Voice' in Composition Pedagogy," *Rhetoric Review* 14, no. 1 (Autumn 1995).

STOP

Lana Turner was fifteen (according to her) or sixteen (according to most sources) on the day that Billy Wilkerson, a journalist with the *Hollywood Reporter*—a writer, not a talent scout—spotted her at the Top Hat Café, gave her his card, and told her to give him a call. Lana had no acting experience.

REWIND

I would worry about you if you pushed yourself into the limelight with this material. Bust foremost, like Lana Turner, the Sweater Girl. All flash, no substance.

Save yourself as a writer.

Save myself for what?

Having come to writing late, (too afraid, too unsure, too concerned that I couldn't find my voice), having labored already for nearly my full complement of "ten years in the cold" once prophesied to apprentice writers by Ted Solotaroff in *Granta*, having published a long string of short pieces that may win awards but don't win me recognition or respect, I don't *want* to put aside my own ambitions. Not once I've found my material.

Renunciation is a part of the writing life.

I am no stranger to renunciation. I love my child without expectation of return. Must I love my work the same way?

Save yourself as a writer. It smacks of saving myself for marriage. There is something illicit, even something erotic in the idea of telling truths about the people we love.

And everybody knows this: Mothers must renounce the erotic.

FAST FORWARD

Later, much later, I read my classmates' written comments. They do not sound like what got said in class. Sometimes that happens in workshops. A ball starts rolling and nobody can stop it. It picks up momentum and so much gets left behind. Now I can see that my classmates liked my writing. They thought I had an important story.

They just didn't know if it could be, or should be, a book. They didn't know because they weren't experienced. None of them had written a book. (The instructors had written books, though, and they thought I should not write this one.)

Later still, I think about the people in that class. Most were daughters. Not one, as I recall it, was the mother of a daughter. Not one.

STOP

Cheryl Crane was arrested and charged with the murder of Johnny Stompanato. Despite confusing evidence—including a lack of fingerprints on the weapon and an absence of blood at the scene—a coroner's inquest ruled it "justifiable homicide," and Cheryl went free. But she and Lana Turner remained alienated for a long time—according to some accounts, for almost forty years, or until her mother's death. Suffering the fallout from a mother's selfish choices undermines a child's trust; witnessing a child's violence—even when that violence seems justified—erodes a mother's hope in the future. And sometimes, in our urgency to protect the people we love, we end up destroying our relationship with them.

REWIND

Writing this will irreparably ruin your relationship with your daughter. I've often wondered whether I'm to blame. Whether that long separation for the first writers' conference was the cause or at least the catalyst for Maia's later anger and anxiety and violence. Her reactions at the time had seemed normal. She had welcomed me home. We'd slipped back into our routines like otters returning to water. The problems hadn't surfaced until later. They had seemed complex, so complex that the psychiatric labels couldn't cover them, so complex that no one cause could be found. But what if the reason had been staring us in the face? What if it was all my fault?

Your story reminds me of one that I want to write, about my friend, the priest who is also a pedophile. When is a child like a pedophile? (You can't portray a pedophile as good in any way. You can't portray a child as bad in any way. People want the simple story.)

Maybe the writer is the pedophile. Abuser. Exploiter.

PLAY

As Maia matured, it became clear that she has what teachers call an "auditory learning style." That is to say, she learns primarily by listening. She also shows a gift for words. Her puns startle and amuse. Her vocabulary rivals that of children twice her age. She reads aloud with enthusiasm and intonation, mimics newscasters and our guests, and can retell a story as told to her, exact in all its parts.

How great a role did those tapes that I made for her play in the development of these strengths?

FAST FORWARD

It takes me almost a year to write this essay. To say that I compose it would imply a calm deliberation I don't feel. Writing this is wrenching. But it's not like pulling teeth. Pulling teeth is a lot easier. At least you know what you are going after. This is more like pulling at entrails. Or untangling a knot. Looking for a thread that I can't find. And every time I do find it, every time I get a purchase, feel a loosening, something interrupts me. So I start. Stop. Start again. Go over what I've already done. Change it. Stop. Change it back.

Sometimes, I am the cause of these interruptions. Me. My own fears. My own worries. My own process and problems and angst. But often my daughter interrupts. She falls from a fence, needs stitches, and her hard-won calm shatters. So improved over the past months, she begins to rage and hit again, so each morning I sit at the computer with bruised forearms and a sense of discouragement. Then she gets a virus and I have to give up my writing hours to care for her. Then I am volunteering in her classroom; then it's her gym day and I need to pick her up early; the next day, she has an appointment with her therapist. That's what it's like.

PLAY

Listening to those tapes, I am struck by the energy in my voice. I'm no actor. But I read with expression, verve, gusto. Individuating each character, from Mortimer, who takes such glee in annoying everybody else, to Shy Charles, who doesn't like to talk. I'm the witch, the princess, the fairy godmother, and the wolf. I sound happy on those tapes. Even when impersonating a growling ogre. What I hear in those tapes is pure, uncomplicated, unconditional love. And that's what my daughter listened to, every night. The nights that I was gone and the nights that I was home. During the day, I may have sounded—*must* have sounded—irritated, exhausted, sarcastic, judgmental, disappointed, even despairing at times. But at night, Maia heard different.

STOP

Stoma. Stompanato. Eerily similar sounds, the one an abbreviated other. Perhaps this irony occurred to Lana Turner as she lay, those last months, on her deathbed. She was known for her sense of humor, so the thought might have tickled her. Tickled—then lodged in her throat, and become an irritation, an annoyance, maybe a sore. Unvoiced.

PLAY

Before my second trip to the conference, I made a new recording. Instead of a tape, I burned a CD, using the soundtrack on the movie software that came with my computer. It was rough, patched together, but passable, although the built-in mike kept cutting out on me and I had to rush through several of the stories. After recording forty minutes or so—poems I'd written for her, songs, a funny story about a boy who calls himself "King of the Blahs"—I realized that, this being a CD, there was lots of room for more. So I downloaded some Robert Munsch books from the web. Authors as popular as Munsch apparently can afford to give their work away. Maia loved the CD. But later she told me, "I wish it was just you on the CD. I like Robert Munsch and I like his stories. But I like your stories better. And I really like to listen to *your* voice."

STOP

Literary critics often speak of "presence" and "codes" and "intertextual discourse" when discussing voice, but writers can scarcely afford to be so theoretical or lofty in their approach. Voice is, to paraphrase Flannery O'Connor, the mud that we use to write.[4]

REWIND

Mama's voices. Plural. Charming mistake, or startling insight? Even on a cheap kids' tape recorder, you can always hear more than one.

RECORD

Like any curious child, Maia liked to play with the buttons on her tape recorder and to experiment with the amplifying feature on its microphone. Parts of those old tapes are blank now, where she has erased them. Parts of them sound with her own words. In her own voice.

4. Steven Schwartz, "Finding a Voice in America," in *Bringing the Devil to His Knees: The Craft of Fiction and the Writing Life*, ed. Charles Baxter and Peter Turchi (Ann Arbor: University of Michigan Press, 2004).

Living in Someone Else's Closet

SUSAN ITO

The first piece I ever wrote about family was a poem about my birth-mother, a year after I'd searched for and found her. I was a senior in college and I was infatuated with this beautiful, charming woman who had given birth to me twenty-one years before, and then given me up for adoption. Her initial response to being discovered was alarm and anger; she had, she said, "put that all behind" her. But after an eight-hour marathon session of talking and sharing photos and stories in a midwestern hotel room, a tentative, tender, secret relationship was born.

She began writing me long letters, adorned with animal stickers, written in perfectly round, bubbly script. She sent me postcards from every family vacation and outing: the state fair, a beach in Mexico, the southwestern desert. She penned compelling stories about trips she took with her husband and their two children (my half-siblings, who knew nothing of my existence). "Maybe next year you'll join us," she wrote, and my heart jumped, reading those words. Next year never came.

The poem that I wrote that year, on a portable electric typewriter, was called "The Closet." The sheet of onionskin paper on which I typed it has long since vanished, but I remember it. I remember writing about how it felt to live in another person's closet, where I could hear the muffled sounds of her life, hear the voices of my half-siblings, but where no one could hear me. I longed to tap out a message on the wall, but I was afraid. Afraid to lose her. Afraid I'd be walled up forever, like the man in the Edgar Allan Poe story "The Cask of Amontillado."

That has been my dilemma from the beginning: needing to write, needing to affirm, to make real my own story, my very life, but being afraid to risk the loss of that relationship. I have struggled with it for decades now.

During that marathon eight-hour "getting to know you" session in 1980, she told me things, things I had been wondering about and longing to understand since I was a child. What had been the circumstances of my birth? Why had she given me away? Who was my birthfather? Who did I look like, where did I come from? I wanted to know it all: I was starving for these details, to fill in the blank spaces of my life, all that had passed before I started life as Susan Ito, a girl who would grow up with Japanese parents in northern New Jersey.

She was not completely forthcoming. After each question, there was a pause, a tight sigh, and a few words. The story emerged in tiny fragments. This is what I came to understand. Her Japanese American family had been uprooted from their California home when she was a child, and relocated in an internment camp in the desert for years. After World War II ended, they were offered a kind of sponsorship, a new beginning, by a church group in the Midwest. They accepted this offer and were enveloped by a small town where there were no other Asian people for hundreds of miles.

My birthmother was not a teenager who accidentally became pregnant. She was nearly thirty years old when I was conceived. She had been so Other, so different, that nobody was brave enough to step away from their European roots to openly court her. So she went underground and had a secret relationship.

This is all she told me. He was married. He had three children close to my age. He was "gregarious, athletic" and "well known in his field." She told me that she was still in touch with him, and had in fact told him I'd found her, and that he had been pleased by the news. She would not tell me his name.

That was more than thirty years ago. The conditions of our ongoing relationship were these: that I not tell anyone known to her that

I was her daughter, and that I not ask further questions about my father. Any time I dared to cross either line, any time I approached either boundary from a hundred yards, the result was an immediate freeze-out. At one point she did not speak to me for six years.

I took those crumbs of story she doled out to me. I obsessed over them, embellished them and tried to grow them into whole narratives that would explain my origins. I started by writing a story about a little Japanese girl in an internment camp, based on a few sentences she had spoken in that hotel room. The story was published; it won a cash prize and was nominated for a Pushcart. I sent a copy to her and I think she was stunned and pleased. Here was her young life, in print.

My plan was to write a novel starting with that little girl in the desert, moving her on to the midwestern town where she was a complete outsider. I would show the progression of her life, the beautifully different high school girl with dozens of friends but no dates. No marriage prospects. I would show her falling in love; I would write the beginning of my life.

I do not know what it is like for people who know their histories, their birth stories; perhaps they take them for granted and never give them a second thought. But to have great gaping holes in the narrative, I think, only fueled my desire to be a writer, to fill in those holes with images and ideas, endless possibilities, anything, anything but a blank spot.

I wrote the sequel to the internment-camp story and that, too was quickly published. That story depicted the family's arrival in the small town, their bewilderment, their otherness. Her response to this one was much less enthusiastic. She saw where this was going. I felt the air between us, thousands of miles, freeze into icy particles. I was stepping into forbidden territory.

That was when my writing went underground. It felt impossible to risk either my relationship with my birthmother or my nascent writing life. I fervently believed that I needed both to survive.

Meeting my birthmother, as fraught and complicated and conditional as it was, had been an amazement for me. Here, for the first time in my life, was a person whose physical self reflected bits of mine back: the shapes of our faces, our lips, our legs, were identical. We were the same height. We had the same very strong eyeglass prescription, the same taste in ice cream, and later on in life, the same high blood pressure. And even though we struggled back in a fierce tug of war over who owned what information, what knowledge, what stories, there was a closeness and an intimacy we shared that I had never known before. We liked to do the same things, go out to interesting and quirky restaurants and eat with our hands. We liked the same books and movies. We could sit up all night and talk.

The mother I grew up with, the mother I live with now, is very different. She has never much liked to talk, isn't much for reading other than cat mysteries, and was adamantly opposed to topics of conversation that strayed far from what was for dinner or what I'd done at school (academically, not socially). We don't look alike or think alike, and we don't like the same kind of ice cream. I have no doubt of her love for me, and she has been the most dedicated of mothers, but I often felt as if she regarded me as a creature from another planet.

When I was thirty, I entered an MFA program and began work on a new novel, a series of interconnected vignettes that combined my imagined history with the fragments she'd shared. In my second year of graduate school, a visiting writer whom I deeply admired told me that the writing was good, but suggested that perhaps I needed a bit of . . . distance from my subject. I was indignant. Distance? She lived two thousand miles away. I had plenty of distance.

I see now, of course, that I had no distance whatsoever. I may as well have still been a fetus floating inside her, for all the distance I had. Every time I wrote a word about my birthmother's life that I knew was unsanctioned, I felt like a thief. I was caught red-handed and terrified. My writing put a great strain on our relationship, because it was something I would never mention. Now I had my own block of silence to match hers. Nor was it something I would share with my adoptive parents, whom I felt I needed to protect from the intensity of my feelings for her. They were already bewildered by my decision to scrap my physical therapy career, something they had been so proud of, had sacrificed so dearly to pay for. And I was abandoning that to become what? A writer?

The library of books in my childhood home consisted of my own packed shelves of children's, then young adult, then volumes of real literature. Books climbed in shelves up to the ceiling, they sprawled over the surfaces of tables and bureaus, and were piled into towers in my closet. Outside my bedroom door, though, there was only one small shelf on the sunporch: a single row of *Reader's Digest* Condensed Books, which came in the mail once a month. I gobbled them like candy.

So yes, they were dismayed when I announced my desire to go to graduate school to get a degree in creative writing. Only when I translated the degree into "English teacher" did they relax.

So I wrote the first draft of my novel, titling it *Filling In the Blanks*, and turned it in as my MFA thesis. I imagined that I would add another hundred pages over the next year, polish it up, and get it published. My second daughter was born a week after I graduated, and when she was ten weeks old I got a full-time job teaching composition at a community college. I worried that if I didn't take that job, I'd never get another opportunity. Do I even have to say that the novel didn't get finished?

Two years later, I picked up the pages of my thesis and was mortified at what I read. How naïve! What . . . lack of distance! I decided to start it again, from the beginning. For three years, I submitted chapters to my writing group. It took me months to develop appropriate camouflage for myself and my family members as I tried to write my story. I added an imaginary brother. I tried various occupations on the parent characters: my fictional father would be a dentist. No, an electrician. No, a groundskeeper. My mother would work in a dingy automobile-tire showroom. My birthmother—I'd make her . . . a calligrapher! I spent months doing research on each of these jobs, scribbling the details of their daily lives. But in the end, the prose felt flat and muffled. I'd dressed everyone up in so much disguise, they could barely move or speak.

I wrote two thousand pages and three drafts of that novel, and never got close to the end.

I decided to turn to others' stories of adoption. Because even if I never could write my own, I was still obsessed with these themes of loss, family and identity. In 1994 I coedited a literary anthology of stories and poems on adoption. I included two of my own pieces, but they were about others' lives, not mine: I realized I wasn't ready to touch that with the proverbial ten-foot pole. I wrote a poem about Albert Einstein's bastard daughter, Lieserl, and a short story about a child my friends had adopted in Nicaragua. My own story remained untold, and when readers and friends asked, I said, "I'm saving that for my novel."

The novel. It had taken on characteristics of what Spalding Gray called The Monster in the Box. I took it out one more time and laid it side by side against an essay I'd written and had published in an anthology of Asian American women. The nonfiction piece felt as if it were about to burst into flame, it was so real. I understood then that fiction was probably not going to be the ideal vehicle for this story.

Thus began my memoir. It was the year I decided to be brave, too, to stand up once and for all and tell my birthmother. I wrote her a letter and told her two things: one, that I was writing a book about our shared story, and two, that I wondered if a certain person, whom my half-sister had mentioned to me once, could possibly be my birth-father. In other words, I named names.

I didn't hear from her for six years. There was enormous fallout. Here I had spent over fifteen years carefully tiptoeing around the landmines, trying not to upset her. But at the same time I was carrying my own bomb, in the form of manuscript pages, and it was strapped to my body. When I told her what I was doing, our relationship detonated.

At first, I was in shock. I couldn't believe she could vanish from my life so completely. Every year since we had met, we had exchanged birthday gifts and wishes in the same month. It was always an enormous joy for me, a healing of our history, to be acknowledged by her on my birthday. Three months after my letter, her birthday came first. I sent her a package and card. No response. Then my birthday came. And went. The mailbox stayed empty. The phone didn't ring. I went into a tailspin of grief and profound loss. My mind started constructing malevolent riddles like, *If the person who gave birth to you wishes you weren't born, do you deserve to be alive?* I spent half a year in a dark, dark place, contemplating suicide. Cliffs overlooking high places began to have a certain appeal. I believe that my six- and two-year-old daughters were all that held me back from the brink.

Time passed. Years, in fact, and with every birthday, I began to understand and believe that I could, in fact, live without her.

And what of the story, the memoir? For years I couldn't bear to look at it. It was too painful. The ending keeps changing. I end it with her disappearance. I end it with my adoptive father's death and the brief sympathy call my birthmother made, when I felt her heart come back to me for an instant. I end it with my adoptive mother's diagnosis with Alzheimer's and her coming to live with our family. I end it and end it. I keep writing it and it never ends.

Some people say that they can't write freely until all the major characters are dead. I just hope I can manage to do it before I'm dead myself.

My husband used to say, "Honey, maybe you'll be like Frank McCourt." Meaning, I'll finally write this when I'm sixty-five, when I've truly gained enough of that distance. It used to fill me with such despair to hear those words. It felt like failure, like endless waiting. But now I think of writing a memoir at sixty-five and it gives me a sense of peace and relief. It says to me, *It will happen. Be patient.*

There have been some recent small shifts in both the writing and in life. I've resumed a cordial, fragile relationship with my birthmother, in the form of infrequent e-mails and brief visits every few years. She says that she's too old to hold on to past angers, and I'm grateful for that. And I've been slipping a few nonfiction pieces out into the world, bits of our story that I'm sure would send her back into oblivion if she knew. I'm careful to never use what the adoption agencies refer to as "identifying information." I'll never publish her name, or even the states where she's lived, but I will say that she's from the Midwest. Is that vague enough? I'm trying to balance holding them both, keeping a tentative contact with her at the same time that I tell my tale. Word by word, it's taking a lifetime, but I'm tapping my way out of the closet.

3
Filling the
Silence

The True Story

KAREN SALYER MCELMURRAY

Why not write a novel? My father asked me that the day I told him I intended to write a memoir about the surrender of my child to adoption in Kentucky in 1973. We were standing in the kitchen in his house in Frankfort, and I remember most how he went on cutting bacon and red peppers and onion into careful little piles.

I don't think I helped anything. I quoted Dorothy Allison on how and why we need stories. Until you write the hardest things, the most difficult things in your life, Allison says, your writing won't be worth a damn.

It would be better for everyone if you just told it like a story, my father said, and he went on making his delicious omelets.

In eastern Kentucky where I grew up, stories were as much a part of the place as the garden beside my grandparents' house. There were Jack Tales. Mountain ballads. *Shady Grove. Barbara Allen.* There were stories about Jenny Wiley, a Floyd County, Kentucky, woman held hostage by Cherokees during the 1800s. But no one talked much about the stories that mattered most to them. A great-aunt of mine named Stella who had to be "kept" at home with her curious visions. My aunt Ruby, who had to be walked across the kitchen floor the time she tried to take her own life. Her visions were of herself as Jesus crucified.

I needed stories, real ones. By day, I sat in a recliner in the living room and went outside only when my mother allowed me onto the confines of a small patio. *Can't you do anything but make a mess?* she'd ask. She dressed me, combed me, and bathed me until I was nearly fourteen years old. Today, I imagine her obsessive rituals of cleanliness kept her safe from some terrible, never-named ghosts of her own childhood. It was stories I turned to for comfort and to transport me beyond that too-clean world.

By day, I read piles of books from the public library. Horse books, dog books, books about the sea. Dostoevsky, Hawthorne, D. H. Lawrence. Books too young, books too old, any book I'd read for hours in the living room recliner where I led my life. By night, stories were my salvation. Each night before she went to bed, my mother, her white gloves heavy with the lotions that soothed her chapped hands, tucked me in, scolded me for kicking the sheets. Later, my parents' voices colliding in the dark, I made up stories. *Captivity tales. Adventures on the ocean. Castles in France.* I was a spinner of wishes, a hero at last.

I loved stories on television about the revolution I saw going on. Haight-Ashbury. Movies about teenagers become hippies become freedom itself. I hit the streets right in my hometown. My friends and I stole speed and downers from our parental medicine cabinets. We bought what we could from Peace Park in the nearest big city. Quaaludes. Black Beauties. Meth. I got my own geographic education from the names for marijuana, purchased from boys ten years older than me. Acapulco Gold. Panama Red. I lived with my father after the divorce, but he was gone often, either to work for state government or to the home of the girlfriend who would soon become my stepmother. I was free of my mother and I was floating. I wanted energy on the run, ecstatic dreams, visions I could taste. My first acid trip ever, I spent hours in a car junkyard at night, talking to the huge eyes I'd seen in a spacecraft that was actually the bed of a Ford pick-up. On speed, I sat for hours in my room and did pencil sketches of my own body. Face. Hands. The narrowness of my hips and belly. Beneath each picture I wrote parts of poems. *Fill me up like wonder. Fill me up like air.* I was so lonely my words were tiny vessels made of clay. In my head I saw them exploding, one by one by one, until I went out into the empty house and found a gun in the drawer of my father's desk. I fired it twice into the backyard and stood there crying.

The night I lost my virginity was not a story like the ones my mother used to read: *Sue Barton, Student Nurse*; *Tammy in Love*. My boyfriend, Jim, and I parked in a grove of trees two miles up from the subdivision where I lived. We left the door of the Plymouth open, so that our feet hung out. I was pinned down by Jim's bulk atop my own anorexic body. He stared down at me, his eyes feverish and frightened. I was frightened, too. On the one hand, it was a status symbol, my deflowering at age fifteen. I'd be hipper, wiser, lean and mean. On the other hand, there were rumors. Buckwheat, a girl in my high school, got pregnant at sixteen and now snuck furtively up and down the halls as if she were perpetually anointed by stray semen and bad luck. Jim and I were both surprised that we'd done it, that it was over so soon.

In the stories my mother told me about sex, it was a duty to be endured. It happened at night, down there, in the body's netherworld. The truth is, I burned inside. Burned when I peed. Burned when I thought about how tough I now was, me, hippie girl with a lover, girl with a lover, girl no more. Then I began to sleep. Slept through classes. Slept when I visited my best friend's house and it was afternoon and we were listening to her books on tape for the blind, fast speed. Usually, I would have been amazed at the sound of ninety-mile-an-hour stories, but those afternoons, I drifted on the couch, my stomach queasy, roiling. *Are you all right?* she asked. I was not all right. Two months passed, then a third, and I knew. I was pregnant. I jumped from chairs, pounded my belly, demanded that this baby, if it was one, leave me forever. By the time I was four months pregnant, it was too late to turn back. I hit the streets again, this time as a runaway.

In the halfway houses and on the streets of Columbia, Missouri, I grew so thin my skin was luminous, scary white, my stomach so transparent, I could have seen my baby's face if I had known how to look. I grew so thin, my body couldn't hold heat. I shivered as I lay in a St. Louis hospital bed and stared, for the first time, at my baby's heart on a monitor. My body, with the son inside that I would give away at birth, was a story so far away words couldn't yet find it.

In her essay "My Vocation," Italian author Natalia Ginzburg says that "we cannot hope to console ourselves for grief by writing." For years, I wrote bad poems. I kept a dream journal. I wrote a story about a girl named Leah Wheeler who is a pregnant runaway who lives on the streets of Columbia, Missouri. I finally wrote a novel, one about a Kentucky coal mining family and a mother who leaves her child behind so she can be a tap dancer. When the novel had been finished for a couple of years, I found myself one day looking at an essay I'd written in graduate school.

The essay was about the women in my mother's family—how my mother fears coal dust on the living room walls, fears any world outside the four walls of her house. I'd written about my aunt's visions of god, my other aunt's terrible bouts of depression, my mother's OCD. And somewhere, in the middle of those pages about those women, I found a few sentences about my own life. I'd described a dream I'd had once, when I was traveling in Crete and sleeping out on a beach at night. I'd described a blond-haired boy who came up out of the sea and walked toward me, touched the top of my head. *It's all right*, he said as he touched me. *I forgive you.*

What I actually wrote during that time, in terms of a new book, were sketches. I wrote about my mother and father and what I knew about their first married year in an apartment in Topeka, Kansas, a place where my mother almost learned to drive and where, after that year, she gave birth to me. I lined my study walls with her photographs—their wedding day, then her pinched, tense face after I was born. I wrote about our lives in Harlan County, where my dad had been a high school math teacher. The more I wrote, the more I remembered. The more I remembered, the harder the questions grew. What, I wanted to know, had caused my mother's descent into fear? Why had she gone back to her parents' house in eastern Kentucky and never left?

It was time, I was beginning to realize, to go deeper. I needed to look not just at the women I'd grown up with, but at the woman I had not yet become. I was a woman who feared intimacy, who wanted children but did not have them, who grew depressed in late June, early July. I was a woman who had begun to wake herself up at night with uterine contractions. I want no children, I'd told friends for years. I wanted to write. But at what cost? "Our capacity to move forward as developing beings rests on a healthy relationship with the past," says Patricia Hampl in her essay "Memory and Imagination." A wall of forgetting stood between me and my own loss.

For the next three years I worked on what later became a memoir called *Surrendered Child: A Birth Mother's Journey*, which is the story of my relinquishment of a child to a state-supported adoption in Kentucky during 1973. As I wrote, I recalled a dream I'd had about the apocalypse during the forty-eight hours of my labor with my son's birth. I recalled the taste of sweet yellow milk from my own breasts, and how my breasts dried and ached and emptied after I'd given him up. In the years after my son's relinquishment, I'd seen him again and again. I'd had dreams about babies trapped in cellars in wartime. Dreams about flowers with the heads of children. Dreams about my own womb opening at night and spilling out warm waters from a faraway ocean. As I wrote a memoir about family—about my own mother, myself as a mother, about the son I'd surrendered—my depression shifted, and so did the way my story was told.

My stories had always been, as a writer friend once described them, a product of "lyric darkness." They waded through themselves, struggled for shape and movement in the dark waters of my own memories. In writing my memoir about family, I began to see how the pieces fit. In a novel I'd written, the main character, at the end of the narrative, rises from the depths of pond water toward sunlight. In the memoir, I rose too. Childhood followed birth, young adulthood followed those years I'd lived with my mother's cleanliness. The narrative moved forward.

And yet the truth is, I have long believed the story, the superstition, that my mother's family repeats, the one about mirrors breaking and the complexities that follow. The truth is, I have cast stones into the still waters, broken the glossy surface of the past.

My particular story has a happy ending. Following the writing and publication of my memoir, *Surrendered Child*, the truly miraculous happened. The son I had envisioned for years, the son I'd conjured in words, came into my life. His then-girlfriend found me on a website, and I met Andrew Cox. My son was a reality.

In the winter of 2002, I visited my mother's house in eastern Kentucky. I took her a copy of my memoir. She sat rifling through the photographs of family at the book's center—the photographs of the son she didn't, until then, know I had. After a while, she laid the book aside, said nothing, studied her face in the cosmetic mirror she keeps on the coffee table. She studied the whiteness of her teeth, the lines beside her eyes.

In the autumn of 2002, I invited my father to a writer's conference in Lexington, Kentucky, where I read a chapter from my book about the day of my son's birth. *There's a lot she doesn't know*, I overhead him whispering to a stranger in the reception line. Later, at home, he stood looking at himself in a mirror in the hall. *You made me look*, he said. *There was so much I should have said, but I didn't know how to look.*

And in the summer of 2003, I visited my son in Tucson, Arizona. We stood together for a long time in front of the same mirror, comparing our noses, our mouths, the likenesses of our faces.

In her essay "The Intelligent Heart," Patricia Foster says that truth-telling in writing can lead us to "stories [that] come from the mystery of unknowable places." I can only say this: I wrote my life, page after page. Most importantly of all, I wrote about my family with the possibility of forgiveness. And while the stories I have yet to tell still exist in the dark woods, on the paths of memory and sometimes confusion, by writing family, I have glimpsed my own way out.

I Might Be Famous

RALPH JAMES SAVARESE

I had just finished a memoir, *Reasonable People*, about adopting a boy
with autism from foster care, a boy said to be profoundly retarded.
The book traced his remarkable journey from an abused three-year-
old to a straight-A, honor-roll student at our local middle school, and
it contained much of what he'd typed on his talking computer from
the age of nine, when he became literate, to the age of twelve, when
the book ended. The final chapter was his, a heartbreaking medita-
tion on his life, replete with longing for those whom he had lost, anger at those (including the teachers at his special school) who had
underestimated his abilities, and reservations about the project to
which he was contributing—and of which he was the subject.

"I'm trying to get used to testing my real self. I'm nervous because
I might possibly be famous. Each day I'm sad and resentful of your
book," he wrote at the beginning of his chapter. In a letter to my
wife's folks that he'd chosen to include, he declared, "Yearn to have
more input into what happens around here: Dad's book, possibly the
house changes." (We were in the midst of a major renovation.) And,
finally, toward the end, he took me to task for how I had represented
his birth mother, a woman with severe alcohol and drug problems
who had lost at least five children to the State. My liberal politics
about poor women had interfered with his experience of this particular poor woman. "You're too nice to her, Dad," he said. "I had a
great fear of her dunking me each day in the water for long times
without letting me breathe in our easy-listening apartment."

I hadn't known, when I wrote the book, that she had flirted with killing him—a fact that devastated me—just as I hadn't known, when my wife and I tried to help her with rehab and a place to live, about the other children she'd abandoned. In many respects, the woman *was* the very essence of the conservative "welfare queen." Upon receiving the chapter, I delighted in my son's disagreement; another view had collided with my own, thereby complicating each. We'd usefully staged the problem of point of view, as fundamental as it is inescapable. Further, I was thrilled that he had taken over the story of his life, that he was now strictly representing himself, apart from his adoptive parents. "It's *My* Story!" read the chapter title—something he had typed in the fourth grade when a peer suggested a change to his "Frosty, the Snowman" narrative. "Don't want help!" he had added through the text-to-voice software. (Sometimes he wants the synthetic voice itself to get angry, to rise above its compulsory modulation.)

The whole point of the book and of the life the three of us had constructed was to show what was possible with respect to family making and autism, especially at the so-called low-functioning end of the spectrum. People assumed that adoption was the last resort of a desperate couple and that no one in their right mind would choose to adopt a significantly disabled child. Call these beliefs the twin shibboleths of blood relations and normalcy. People similarly assumed a range of noxious things about autism. The reigning "theory of mind" hypothesis, which held that Autistics have no awareness of self or others and are likely retarded, had done great damage.

It was time for new ideas, time to apply the concept of diversity to the field of neurology, time to allow Autistics to write back to the empire of science. Can the subaltern speak or, rather, type? You bet. The book literally embodied the move from representation to self-representation that is such a hallmark of identity politics. I was proud of our achievement, and I saw the book as a kind of activism, the work of a public intellectual. My son, too, saw it as activism—what he calls "political freedom fighting." I had given him the power to veto its publication, but he chose not to, despite his obvious ambivalence. "No," he typed. "Want to help other poor kids and autistic kids."

And so, I went forward, though I still worried about exposing my son, however laudatory the purpose. This wasn't the case of a writer who, like David Sedaris, exploits his family for personal gain, or so I told myself. William Faulkner once said, "The 'Ode on a Grecian Urn' is worth any number of old ladies." He was trying to justify the betrayal of one's own mother for the glories of art. I had begun my book as an act of advocacy on behalf of those who literally don't have a voice. When my son began to read and to type, my vision of the book changed; I knew I had to incorporate his words and end with a chapter by him. These salutary events made for a better story—both politically and aesthetically.

But did this better story end up impugning me? Was I just a subtler, more insidious Faulkner, protected from the most obvious charge of exploitation by my do-gooder agenda, which had proved the autism experts wrong? I really can't answer this question, except to say that I knew how good a story I had, and I wanted, desperately wanted, to tell it. I am a writer, after all. Art, like politics, appropriates things, and perhaps when children are involved more restraint is necessary.

Not two weeks after sending the completed manuscript to the publisher, I had a panic attack. I had been watching a rerun of one of my favorite shows: *Six Feet Under*. In this particular episode, the girlfriend of the straight mortician brother speaks of the best-selling book that her psychologist father had written about her when she was young— she had been something of a troubled genius. The book had messed her up bad, as we like to say colloquially. Each year at school, it literally preceded her, became the filter through which her teachers and schoolmates viewed her. She'd spent her life running away from it. Of course, I immediately thought of my son—of the book he might spend years running away from. The character's father was so outrageously exploitative that I at once told myself, "You're not him" and "You're him."

Now, my book was far from a bestseller, but it did do well, and we did appear in the national media: *Newsweek*, NPR's *The Diane Rehm Show*, ABC's *Nightly News with Charles Gibson*, CNN's *Anderson Cooper*

360. My son *is* famous, especially in autism circles. He gets invited to speak at conferences all over the country. The first time a stranger approached him in the grocery store, he typed, "Fame is scary," and after a presentation he usually heads for the exit before the crowd descends. (As a culture, we're so far from radically rethinking "low-functioning" autism that the shock of a nonspeaking Autie who types to communicate has people behaving as if he were E.T. "Can I touch him?" someone actually asked.)

In the short run, such renown has been beneficial. It's created opportunities for him and given him standing in our community. It's provided a platform for his cause: namely, a better life for Autistics. In an interview with Dr. Sanjay Gupta on CNN, he announced a desire to hold an autism summit, a summit run *by* Autistics. When asked what sort of issues he wanted to organize about, he replied, "Defining ourselves." Later, when Gupta asked if autism should be treated, he wittily remarked, "Yes, treated with respect." How much better to have this young man representing autism than a hysterical parent or pathologizing doctor?

And yet, the book was extremely intimate. It recounted in great detail my son's abandonment, his separation from his birth sister when he was placed in foster care (because his birth father wouldn't parent a child with a disability), his brutal beating and sexual abuse in his first foster home, his inclusion in a regular school, his battle with posttraumatic stress disorder, his growing recognition of the nature of his difference and the inhospitable society in which he would have to make his way, his long-awaited yet troubled reunion with his sister, whom he needed to reject. All of this was heartbreaking stuff, very personal.

And because my son uses a computer to communicate, there existed a record of his responses to these events, not only his responses but entire conversations with his parents, his doctors, his therapists, his school teachers, his friends, his sister—you name it. A life, or at least its languaged moments, stored forever, conveniently retrievable. No conceit of "remembered" dialogue in this memoir project; rather, the real thing: actual dialogue. This fact made the book seem even more intimate and, thus, even more like a violation of my son's privacy. At the same time, the rich interior that these faithfully documented conversations revealed pushed back against the dominant cognitive paradigm, which insisted that Autistics are incapable of sophisticated self-reflection.

As if the issue of publication weren't thorny enough, the memoir also exposed the lives of other people, even as it took the necessary precautions to conceal their identities. You learn, for example, that my son's birth father was HIV positive, that his new wife threatened to leave him if he chose to parent his son and for years prevented visits between the two siblings. You learn about the child welfare workers who failed to protect a nonspeaking toddler in foster care and about the foster mother under whose very nose the most heinous physical and sexual abuse took place. You learn as well about the principal of the center school who sought to undermine my son's adoption because she disapproved of inclusion and maintained that we just wanted him as a research guinea pig (my wife works in the field of inclusive education and had butted heads with her over the placements of other kids). You learn about my own alienation from my father and sister, whom I regarded as grotesquely insensitive and materialistic. And you learn about my nephew's death from brain cancer and the enormous emotional difficulties that my brother and his wife faced. What right did I have to any of this "material"?

In my pen of pens, I believe that a noble political aim *can* justify the appropriation of others' lives, so long as a writer stages the problem of point of view in all of its vexing complexity. And yet, I want such appropriations to be aesthetically pleasing—I want them for Art—and in this respect I haven't distinguished my motivation from Mr. Faulkner's. People end up being used, and their privacy invaded, either way. But isn't the world positively desperate for something like my son's story? Consider the following exchange between him and my sister-in-law. Look how nicely it shapes the project of compassionate humanity to which we all tell ourselves we are committed. Look how it prompts people to rethink what is possible—both individually and as a society.

I had been teaching my son the word *reasonable*, as in how reasonable it was to insist that I wear the same black outfit to work each morning—perseveration is a common autistic challenge—when he redeployed it in a startling manner, the usage nearly from another planet. Still distraught about her son's death and visiting us in Iowa for Thanksgiving, my sister-in-law was particularly withdrawn that weekend until my son took her by the hand and typed, "Do you have reasonable people to help you with your hurt?" He then followed it up with, "It makes me reasonably happy to see you reasonably happy." The boy who had lost everyone was reaching out to his aunt, telling her it was possible to go on, to feel better, if not perfectly at peace. She smiled, printed off his words and put them in her pocketbook. On the bad days, the really bad days, she'd pull them out, we later learned, and read them, accepting the consolation of sorrow's curly-haired veteran.

I've come to no definitive conclusions about what I did or what other writers should do. I take some pride in the fact that my book confronts the dilemmas of experience and doesn't try to resolve them. In this way, these dilemmas resonate with the dilemmas of publication. Sometimes I think in our celebrity-crazed culture that memoir ought to be avoided altogether. Why go public with a life when to do so is to ask, almost necessarily, for Andy Warhol's hand? While I fear that my book, which presents an inevitable slanting of experience, has become *the* story of my son's past, I fear more that it has been appropriated by the media machine and turned into a spectacle. A small spectacle to be sure, but a spectacle nonetheless. Experience increasingly longs for something other than a web cam or memoirist. The status of testimony to which so many memoirs of personal injury aspire might best be served by silence or some private expression of grief.

A Spell against Sorrow

Writing My Father In

JUDITH ORTIZ COFER

Hoy recuerdo a los muertos de mi casa.
Al que se fue por unas horas
y nadie sabe en qué silencio entró.
OCTAVIO PAZ, *Elegía Interrumpida*

THE FLOOD: A FAMILY CUENTO

A few months after my father was born, while his mother was still recovering from a difficult delivery with only her other young children for company, on a day when her husband was out "de fiesta" with his drinking compañeros, a flash flood inundated the house. As the water poured in, my grandmother placed her terrified infant in a shallow tin tub and let him float around the rooms as she went after her other children, who had climbed up on a table and were screaming for her. By the time she was able to catch the tub carrying my father, it was already heading toward the front door, where he would have plunged into the raging waters outside. The way Abuela told it, the baby would not be pried out of his tiny vessel; his strong little fingers grasped the sides with such incredible determination that she'd had to wait until finally, in exhaustion, he let go. She held him to her breast to try to calm him, but he rejected her offering of milk. The promise of maternal nourishment and security was never again enough for him. He kept his eyes and hands on the bottle while he fed, and his fingers automatically wrapped around the bars of his crib even in his sleep, so that he was always anchored, always tied to someone or something.

137

Someone once commented that my work is riddled with the absence of my father. It is true that in the past, he has only made infrequent, passing appearances in my work. In fact, the vacuum left by his absence in my life made such an impact on my psyche and on my imagination, that to this day, I often feel that at the core of my art there is a whirlpool of contradictory emotions I must approach with care; I must always beware of the secret place where he resides within me, for it is also where grief will lay its trap, blocking my imagination.

My father was in the navy, a reluctant voyager who was away making a good living so we could have a home, who forfeited his own life of the mind so we could get an education. Although absent, he was the final authority on everything, the one whose praise we sought and whose return we both feared and desired. He possessed us with his unfulfilled dreams. I was influenced by his needs more than my own because he was the Byronic hero of my early life. He rarely smiled; his sadness walked in and out of our lives with his arrivals and departures. He was known as *un hombre muy serio* to our friends: one of the few Puerto Rican men in my small world of the barrio who did not, at least occasionally, drink, dance, or play dominoes. These may seem like the typical trivial pursuits of Latinos everywhere, but they were markers in my young mind that something was amiss. He was not like the other men I knew, some good, some not, all of whom seemed to accept their ordinary lives during the work week, and yet managed to socialize their problems away on weekends. My father longed for things he sometimes named: our safety, well-being, financial security, and most of all, the education he wanted for my brother and me. An A student in high school, with ambitions to earn a university degree, he'd had to abandon his goals due to the demands of an early marriage and children, and he yearned for things he left unnamed to the end of his life—dreams and hopes that now, as the heir to his story, I must relive, or I will end my days with the hole in my heart that is the memory of father.

All my life I listened hungrily for family stories of my father, especially the *cuentos* about his childhood my abuela told and retold when she stayed with us during my father's long Navy tours; she told them by rote, as if she were a bard in charge of the family's oral history. She had stories about all her six children, especially my father, her youngest, that sometimes sounded like morality tales. Each story was meant to reveal each child's *destino*. I understood, even at an early age, that the stories were as much family myth as they were history, yet even then I needed to see my morose father as the baby in his mother's arms, as the handsome teenager, as the studious young man who was also a gifted baseball player, whom my mother described as an apparition on the baseball diamond, his sandy blond hair and gold-rimmed glasses sparkling in the sun, setting him apart from all the other boys. I also wanted to imagine him joyous at the birth of his own children, us. I wanted to know that at some earlier time before I started to be aware of his melancholy, he had been happy.

Later, as I matured, I had to learn forgive him for imposing his darkness over my childhood, and for the possessiveness and vigilance that cast a dark shadow over my early adulthood. It helped me to see him as the frightened baby in the washtub, grasping hard at the things that meant security to him, so they would not float away from him. In some key ways this is an apt image for what I do as a writer: I hold on for dear life to the stories that keep me anchored, and to the images that are markers and beacons pointing the way home. Listening to the storytellers in my family was like looking through a fantasy family album: each speaker got to choose the angle, the light, as well as the positions occupied by each of the figures in their individual frames. I saw how the same image could be, and often was, reimagined when the "camera" changed hands. Perhaps this is how I began to understand that the teller holds the power, and that, while she is telling it, the story belongs to her.

I understood my father's hungry heart too late. He was gone by the time I knew why *I* was unable to trust happiness, or to ever be fully satisfied with my accomplishments—I still needed his approval as an adult, but for a long time, I was too angry to let him know how much I cared. Although I have a much easier life than he could have ever imagined, and mainly thanks to his insistence that I become an educated woman, I have inherited his *tristeza*. In the few weeks a year he got to have a home life with us, time that was spent preparing us for his leaving again for months at a time, he became a living reminder of the inevitable end of good things such as security, the comfort of family and friends. The combination of relief and anger I felt on his departures provided me with enough guilt to last me a lifetime. I was happy to have the gray fog of his depression dissipate from our apartment. I was glad I did not have to answer his softly spoken, but insistent, interrogations about my most ordinary activities. I was glad my mother felt free to play her salsa albums loud again, and sing along with them. It was always as if we had been observing *luto* in our house, and the period of mourning was finally over. I also hated his departures because then I would be charged with being the family's translator and records-keeper, for he'd want to know every detail of what he would miss out on while doing his duty as engineer in the dark and claustrophobic boiler rooms of a navy cargo ship, with only his imagined fears for us as company. I was in charge not only of translating for my mother, but also of taking notes on meetings with teachers, principals, doctors, and even the postman, so that I could answer my father's questions about how our ordinary daily dilemmas and confrontations with the English-speaking world were resolved, or were not, and if not, what I had failed to make clear to the others, the ones outside our little Spanish-speaking circle, who never really understood our needs. The imperative to keep *la familia* safe entailed my becoming fully bilingual quickly, and I suspected, also clairvoyant. I had to be able to see future threats so I could overcome them, to have words available to protect us from potential manipulations by people who thought all non–English speakers were also nonthinkers. Beware of salespeople at the door. Beware of word tricks. *Free* doesn't always mean *gratis*. Whenever he left us for his time at sea, my father deposited his keys to the car and the house, and his suspicions and fears, in my hands. I felt the burden of too much responsibility at too early an age, but then there was also the gift he gave me, which I could not recognize then, of valuing my mind and nurturing my need for an education. I was not ever asked to spend my time on housework or duties of any kind that would take me away from my books for too long; instead I was given the mandate to learn, to empower myself through language. But for most of those years, I mainly felt the weight of his authority, and I resented him for making me the guardian of all *he* needed and valued.

And then, just as I was beginning to awaken from the self-absorption of my teenage years and the collapse of linear time between college, early marriage, and the birth of my child—which all seemed to happen at an impossibly accelerated speed, before I could stop and forgive myself and him for the years I spent resenting his rules and my role as my family's public face and thus the adult too early in my life—my father died in an inexplicable collision of his car with an embankment wall. The most methodical, careful driver I have ever known ran into a six-foot wall directly in front of him. He either did not see the wall, or the wall called to him. I am certain we each have our necessary version of the story. I have often asked myself if his sadness finally become unbearable. He would have been ashamed to have admitted it. Now I would certainly have seen through his tough façade and found the scared little boy still trying to survive the flood. I would recognize it because I have inherited *la tristeza* he carried down the highway and into that wall, but my art is the levee that saves me from drowning in the murky water on the other side, and it has held so far.

Yet it wasn't even then, immediately after my father's death, that I realized I had not gotten his vision of himself in our lives, that I could never know the "truth" about him as he saw it himself, that only by writing it would I know how his life narrative has shaped mine. I finally see that it was the role he assigned me as interpreter of American reality for my family that prepared me to be the strong storyteller. But I left him out of my *cuentos* too often. He was the painful omission.

PERDER: TO LOSE

I have always been able literally to abandon myself to my thoughts. Time stops for me while I relive the past and imagine alternate lives so that I can get at the thing that I must know. Obsession is a great technique for a writer. If I don't write about *this* idea, *this* memory, *this* image, the one that has been gestating in my head for months, perhaps even years, but is now clamoring to be born, I will lose it, and I will lose out on any truth it could have yielded.

For me, the poem, the story, is not born when I will it, but when *it's* ready. Then it kicks me from the inside, shakes my diaphragm like the walls of a bone jail, makes me a night walker, a pacer, restless and unsatisfied until it is down on the page.

I set about the task of retrieving memory and emotion armed with a poet's tools. I begin collecting images, words, sounds, all that I can retrieve from the past. I trust the facts to follow the scent of memory.

I go through my usual ritual of self-interrogation early in the morning, in the dark, in my rocker. This is where I will do my recollection before I plunge into the story. The rocker is necessary to my writing ritual. It is the only piece of furniture I brought to my writing space from my house. It had been in our first apartment when I had my daughter. It is where I nursed her and comforted her, and where I sat as a busy young wife, mother, and teacher late into the night wondering if I would ever get to write my poems. It is now where I sit to meditate, and to plan my work. It is made of hemp, woven tight, but yielding. It gives a bit under my bottom. But these days it has a different, less pronounced indentation than before, different than the deep one made by the mother and child weight.

After a pot of coffee and much introspection, I feel disconnected enough from my body and my earthly concerns that I can finally face the blank page. Today what I am thinking is this: my life is a wavy line suspended between two poles. At one end there is a girl and her family I remember through metaphors for loss and alienation, and on the other, the one I sometimes call me, myself, or I in essays and memoir, but whom I do not know as well. She is the one I cannot treat as objectively as the other, for I am too close to the subject. If I write about my family I have to tell the story as I see it through this lens, a glass that is both refractive and reflective. I write what I see, not necessarily what I saw. I tell myself this: my life has contained the lives of others, and has been touched, enriched, damaged, shaped, and changed, for better and for worse, by others' lives. But is my imagining their versions of my story genuinely justifiable, or an invasion? Do I have a right to it all?

Yes, I believe I have the right and the obligation to write my story as fully as I can, and that means incorporating my father's, for I am in his story and he is in mine.

CASTING A SPELL AGAINST SORROW

It may have been the revelation that I had to be the one to tell his story in order to find mine that led me to write my first poems, for it was soon after his death that I dedicated part of each of my days to writing; although, the human brain being what it is, the pain of losing him kept me from writing about him for many years. The forgetting spell was finally broken when I wrote this poem:

Absolution in the New Year

The decade is over, time to begin forgiving
old sins. Thirteen years since your death
on a Florida interstate—and again
a dream of an old wrong. Last night I slept
through the turning of the year,
                  I was fifteen
and back on the day I hated you most: when
in a patriarchal fury at my sullen
keeping of myself to myself,
and convinced I was turning into a Jezebel,
you searched my room for evidence
of a secret other life. You found my diary
under the mattress and, taking it to the kitchen,
examined it under harsh light.
                You read
about my childish fantasies of flight—yes—
from your tyrannical vigilance
and, in the last few pages, of my first love,

almost all imagination.
I suffered
biblical torments as you turned the pages. Unworthy,
exposed before your eyes. I wondered where
I would go, if you should cast me out
of our garden of thorns, but I swore, that day,
my faith to the inviolable self.
Later,
when Mother came in to offer me
a cup of consolation tea, her vague justifications
of "man's ways," and to return the profaned book,
I tore and crumpled each page, and left them
on the floor for her to sweep.
To this day
I cannot leave my notebooks open anywhere:
and I hide my secrets in poems.
A new year begins.
I am almost your age. And I can almost understand
your anger then—caught as you were—in a poor man's trap,
you needed to own, at least our souls.
For this sin of pride, I absolve you, Father.

And more:
If I could travel to your grave today,
I'd take my books of poetry as an offering
to your starved spirit
that fed on my dreams in those days.

I'd place poems on your stone marker,
over the part of your name we share,
over the brief span of your years (1933–1976),
like a Chinese daughter who brings a bowl of rice
and a letter to set on fire—a message
to be delivered by the wind: Father

here is more for you to read.

Take all you desire of my words. Read
until you've had your fill.
Then rest in peace.

There is more where this came from.[1]

AND MORE WHERE THIS CAME FROM

A few weeks before he died, as I was preparing to start graduate
school in English, I had been talking to my parents about writing a
book someday. My mother suggested I wait until I had a story to tell.
I had not lived enough yet, she said. It wasn't until years later, when
I allowed memories of my father to flood my conscious mind, that
I remembered his words to me on that same day, "Why don't you
write my story?" he said. "I have many stories I can tell you." And
my mother, being the family comedian as well as the keeper of family stories now that grandmother was gone, wagged a mock-warning
finger at him, "Some of your *cuentos* are better kept secret, *Querido*."
She may have been warning him not to burden me with sad old stories, or perhaps reminding him of his womanizing days at the start
of their marriage, stories she would tell me in her own time, from
her perspective as the offended party, and so may have been protect-
ing her narrative territory. A look passed between them that changed
the course of the conversation. I can't recall whether he answered
her. Probably not. His words had been directed only at me, and I
choose to believe that it was my father's final unfulfilled wish that
his story be told. Why? I believe that it is a universal yearning to not
be forgotten. I have always regretted the missed opportunity offered
me that day. I have made it my goal to imagine what my father would
have told me, had I been ready to listen to him.

HOW IT BEGINS

"Why don't you tell my story?" my father once asked me.

---

1. Judith Ortiz Cofer, "Absolution in the New Year," in *The Latin Deli: Prose and Poetry* (Athens: University of Georgia Press, 1993).

Things We Don't Talk About

AARON RAZ LINK

There's an essay on my desk. I wrote it a year ago and it's been sitting on my desk ever since. I used to open my computer, read the essay again, and make revisions. Recently, however, I've declared a unilateral revision freeze. The problem isn't that the essay is poorly structured or badly written. The problem is that in just over four thousand words (at last revision) this essay manages to reveal personal information about myself, my mother, her husband, my brother, my sister-in-law, two nieces, my cousin, his wife, their two children, and both my major romantic partners. Most of these people don't have pets, or I'd really be in trouble. The name of the essay is "Things We Don't Talk About."

Perhaps I should know better. Not too many years ago, I wrote a collaborative memoir with Hilda Raz called *What Becomes You*. Before signing a publication contract with the University of Nebraska Press, I gave copies of the manuscript to members of my family; it seemed fair to give them the chance to offer their responses while our options for revision were still open. Since the subject of the book was my sex change, I had some worries. My essays contained reinventions of our shared history, stinging indictments of some treasured popular beliefs about men and women, a lot of comedy, and detailed descriptions of my genitals. Since my coauthor is also my mother, the haunting specter of "what to tell Mom" had already been laid to rest; in some ways, this existential dilemma of every avant-garde was already the subject of the book. As it turned out,

146

the closest I came to a permanent rift with my brother was over the appropriate word to use when describing his residence: "townhouse" or "townhome."

You just never know.

The architect Ludwig Mies van der Rohe is often quoted as saying, "God is in the details." In struggling with my brother over the exact and proper word for his place in a redeveloping inner-city neighborhood, I began to see him as a smart and sensitive reader responding to a story I was telling about social class. I gave him the gift of revision (you'll have to read the book to find out which word we chose). He gave me the gift of a larger kind of re-vision: a way to understand what I was trying to write about, how one particular story might be read differently by different readers, and ultimately why writing might matter. In the exchange, I believe we both began to realize the deep and lasting tensions between public stories—which speak to our collective social patterns—and personal ones, which describe the complex relationship between one person's options and their choices.

Like architects, writers mark borders separating personal spaces from public ones. A writer working with family materials stands in a liminal space where *my* story meets *your* story, meets the reader's story, and becomes *our* story. Before I became a writer, I was a historian working in public museums. As a result, I see that *family* assembles our individual stories together to form larger stories, which are assembled together to become the fabric we call *culture* and *history*. This process gives each of us some sense of belonging to a larger world. The stories themselves provide the explanations we are given for the shapes and meanings of our lives. This is why I am willing, as a writer, to enter the zones of tension that surround family stories. Our individual stories connect, but often where they meet, the exposed ends don't line up. In Harlem, my brother's place seemed to me a part of the edifice of *culture* and *history*. Odd, itinerant lives like mine seemed marginal events happening outside these beautiful buildings. But my odd itinerant life has made me a writer, the builder of pages in which my brother's place is outside, his stories told by me and marginal to mine.

In writing about family, the simple explanations we hold onto often fall away. Losing them can be an uncomfortable process. I think my brother and I both had to realize that at any moment, the ways we are represented can be easily altered by revision—in our circumstances, or in the ways they're framed. What remains are two human beings and the stories we can tell. Thank God, their details do not always agree. That's why writing matters.

My first student writers slept under bridges or in homeless shelters; they knew they could survive outside, but not without trying to make sense of and communicate their experiences: a writer's job. Every couple of weeks, we'd go together to see a movie of their choice. Afterward, we'd discuss. In the process, I learned more about shape-shifting demon mummy kings and zombie robot aliens than I ever really wanted to know. At some point, however, I began to notice that all the movies my students wanted to see featured characters who reflected their lives—characters with skin colors and family relationships as varied as their own. At this point I started to pay better attention. The day they finally found a "serious" movie in which they saw their own lives reflected was a grim one. We sat afterward in silence until my students began to challenge the ending they'd been given.

One person said, "Stories about people like us shouldn't always come to a bad end."

Because I'm a writer, my answer was that every story is a work in progress; if you don't like the end you've been given, you get to make new ones. In *I Could Tell You Stories: Sojourns in the Land of Memory*, Patricia Hampl writes: "If we refuse to do the work of creating this personal version of the past, someone else will do it for us. That is a scary political fact." My students knew human truths behind Hampl's use of the word *political*; they shared their stories with me, and because these stories helped me build a working life as a writer, I pass one on to you. We have a tendency to warn one another of dire fates that will befall us if we leave home, if we move out of our old buildings, go into new neighborhoods, talk to strangers. But we can do those things anyway. We might find our way to good ends.

My faith that writing matters—that writing is a way for us to reimagine our lives and literally change our culture and history—has seen me through many dark nights and Wednesday afternoons of the soul. This kind of deep commitment to the ethics of writing looks great on paper. The writer is fearless; damn the torpedoes, full speed ahead. But the human being is not so sure.

In *The Half-Life of an American Essayist*, the writer Arthur Krystal describes a world of writing I knew growing up: "The only thing that mattered was the life of the mind, and everything relevant to that life—God, sex, politics, society—had to pass through the centrifuge of literature." He quotes Anatole Broyard: "We didn't simply read books; we became them. We took them into ourselves and made them into our histories."

In the seventh grade, I'd felt encouraged to read *Fahrenheit 451*, a science-fiction novel by Ray Bradbury about a world in which all books are burned. But I'd felt encouraged to read it only secretly, hidden behind a book of more visible architectural weight, something I believed was about *history* or *culture*. My encouragement came from the way my English teacher had showed us a film made from Bradbury's book by the famous director François Truffaut. At the end of the film the hero stumbles into a scene of salvation. People are walking slowly through a garden in a fall of snow, speaking familiar words. Each has perfectly memorized a single great work of literature, taking it into themselves and making it part of their history. The people have become books. I fell in love with this scene. It reminded me of my family.

My mother is an editor; though she's also a poet, she devoted much of her professional life to one magazine, the literary journal *Prairie Schooner*. My father became a bibliographer, an obscure, vital job preserving the history and integrity of published writing. He spent fifteen years on the work of one writer, Willa Cather. My brother does not describe his place of residence in his own words because—though he is also a composer of original music—his writing so far has been devoted to the composer Elliott Carter.

For my own part, I took in books ferociously and mostly without discrimination. However, I failed to become a book. Perhaps I lacked focus. However, like my students much later, I sometimes found that the process of taking other people's stories into myself gave me indigestion. Many writers are less able to tolerate that kind of indigestion than Anatole Broyard, and our intolerance opened up another world of writing. So I fell out of love with literature, and into love with theoretical writing, which pays attention to the ways *history* and *culture* are also stories, and does not demand that our thoughts about God, sex, politics, and society be revealed only through appropriate quotes from famous literary figures. This kind of writing gave me a way to imagine coming out from behind the books where I had hidden my own stories, to tell them myself. I wanted my own story to be one worth saving. Many of us were uncomfortable with the ways our lives were absent from the books we'd been invited to become, and I read many authors who wrote about the problem.

Though I'd fallen in love with theoretical writing, the judgments of cultural theorists about the meaning and value of my family's stories left me unsatisfied. In his essay "The Age of Criticism," the poet Randall Jarrell once wrote that criticism "has now become, for a good many people, almost what a work of art exists for: the animals come up to Adam and Eve and are named." I have come to agree. I see no value in forgetting the stories we've been given in order to remember a substitute system of labels. I believe in stories more than in the changing names we give them. But as I watched my family saving other people's stories by becoming them, I still wondered who would remember my family.

Randall Jarrell is a quotable famous literary figure. He also wrote one of my favorite books when I was a kid, a tale my mother brought me called *The Bat-Poet*. It's about a bat who first discovers loneliness, then insomnia, then that light could be quite wonderful, and then that he wasn't happy being in the dark all the time. Eventually, he becomes a writer.

Like my first students and Randall Jarrell, my mother and I wrote because we needed to understand and communicate our experiences. We wrote together about my sex change for all the human reasons people write: to know ourselves, to know each other, to share our knowledge, correct errors, respond to our critics, make a social contribution, make ourselves look good, have a good time, practice our craft. The idea of building personal narratives from our own lives, however, brought up the clear and present danger of trying to justify our lives or explain our family. One thing I had learned from theory and criticism was that justifying yourself is a hopeless task. So I did what any normal, sensible, reasonable person would do under the circumstances: I stopped writing.

I was rescued by two epiphanies. While avoiding work on our book, I watched a lot of smart and articulate theorists writing passionately about experiences that were clearly meaningful to them. I saw gay men writing about lesbians, lesbians writing about transsexual men, Asian Americans writing about African Americans, separatist feminists writing about men, folks from big cities writing about folks from small towns, transsexual men writing about transsexual women. I didn't see any of them writing about the experiences that were specifically their own. And I realized Patricia Hampl's statement is also true in the other direction: if you refuse to do the work of creating your own personal vision of the past, you will do it for someone else.

This, too, is a scary political fact. If you refuse to look in the mirror, you will never know when you are looking at another human being and seeing only yourself.

So I stopped being uncomfortable with my choice to write about my own life and family. I put down the books of theory as well as the books of literature behind which I had been hiding a story—our own—and started finding a way to write it.

Meanwhile, theater taught me that you can see your audience as enemies or friends. If you see them as enemies, not only will they come to dislike you and your fellow players, but you will also find yourself unable to work. As my teachers pointed out, no one wants you to succeed more than the human being who has gone out on a rainy night and put down a piece of their paycheck to find out what you have to say. No one is more eager to laugh at your jokes, believe you are brilliant, insightful, moving, and wise. Readers, in other words, are like family. We trust perfect strangers with our thoughts, feelings, words, with our brothers, sisters, lovers, best friends, parents, children. We do it because we can. As impossible as it seems, this is after all how we create families as well as books. Trust each other.

The writer is fearless; damn the torpedoes, full speed ahead. The human being is not so sure.

Here are some things I tell myself.

I fear writing about family is an exercise in irrelevance, because our family stories matter to no one but us. But "us" makes sense only in a larger context: who is us? Who isn't us? What's the difference, and who says so? The discipline of writing family stories is to make connections between *history* and *culture* and lived experience, and between that lived experience and text. When we do this job, writer and reader are searching together for knowledge that can be tasted and touched, smelled and held, for truths made of something more tangible than convenience, consensus, or politics. To connect personal experience and the written word is also to teach ourselves and one another that neither truth nor text can be absolute. Many family stories are about survival, the most relevant subject I know. Yet one person's—or generation's—prescription for survival may be another's salvation, doom, or joke. So in writing about family, we practice the art of becoming flexible enough to encounter any situation, any story, face to face. This rigid flexibility is my personal prescription not only for good writing, but also for human happiness.

I fear writing about my own family. At an Associated Writing Programs conference I listened to a teacher define bad nonfiction as "stories about blood relatives and body parts." I wince, because this description can be applied to my own book, but I'd also note that this category includes survivor's accounts of genocide, war, reconciliation. Trained as a historian, I wonder what kind of writing *isn't* influenced by family stories, and I think about what can happen when we decide to deny our actual sources—to believe nonfiction can exist without relatives or actual bodies. A recent spate of spurious memoirs (all about "taboo" experiences of body and family) makes me wonder what happens to writing—and to us as readers and writers—when we decide to believe that there are sexy and serious, illicit and proper subjects for writing. Who prospers when one group of people must display their bodies and relatives while another cannot, when one group is considered sexy (profitable), illicit, and egotistical, while another is considered serious (boring), proper, and historically important? Certainly not families like mine and yours, which tend to include people in neither category, or both.

At another conference, I heard wise and well-known writers speak of the need to respect silence, to acknowledge the importance of both social boundaries and personal shame. Certainly it can be awkward to write about sex change. In my parents' youth, mentioning divorce and birth control were similar taboos. Go a little further back, and we mustn't write about labor unions, vegetarians, or knees. I also note that social boundaries and personal shame could have easily silenced writers like James Baldwin, George Eliot, Audre Lorde, Jan Morris, Sherman Alexie, Gloria Steinem, Frederick Douglass, Primo Levi, Quentin Crisp. As a writer, I gain strength and purpose from my association with these names; I too am working in the territory of shifting personal and social boundaries. One change the Internet has made in the lives of writers is that, for the first time, millions of people putting their personal lives online are sharing this territory with us.

Yet I am still afraid. Those of us who have been without authority in one situation or another (and that is probably all of us) know how other people's shame can become a weapon directed at us. Telling our truths may mean losing our jobs, our safety, our freedom. We are often silenced as writers because each day we see vividly how much we have to lose.

And I fear what is most difficult to acknowledge: that the moral high ground I use to reassure myself is an illusion. In writing about my family, I fear I am representing other people in shapes convenient to my purposes but false to their lives—in Hampl's terms, I'm creating their personal visions of the past for them.

No matter how close we are to our families, we can't really know one another's lives. However, when we write nonfiction for publication, we have to choose how to represent those lives in print. In *What Becomes You*, the character of the mother is also my mother, Hilda Raz. I can't believe it suited her purposes as a human being to be represented to the public as naïve and sometimes prejudiced. However, she is also a ferociously good writer and the coauthor of the book, and it suited the book's purposes. Someone in the story needs to ask basic questions, express discomfort, and experience the wonder at the transformation of our lives that we hope our readers will share. That she actually did so in life as well as on the page is part of what makes *What Becomes You* a work of nonfiction.

The astronomer Galileo once explained his theory of the planets to his friend Maffeo Barberini, in a conversation so illuminating he later used it as the basis for his book *Dialogue Concerning the Two Chief Systems of the World*. Writing the text as a conversation between a knowledgeable character and an ignorant one was great for the book. Seeing himself in print as a character called Simplicio (roughly, "Fool") was not so great for Maffeo Barberini, who by then was the Pope. Also not so great for Galileo, who got to have an equally interesting conversation with the Spanish Inquisition. Of course, this story might have ended somewhat differently if His Holiness had been Galileo's mom, and coauthor of his book.

In personal writing there are sins of omission as well as commission. When I showed my father the manuscript of *What Becomes You*, I believe what he read was difficult for him. I had carefully avoided writing about my father at any length, for while he has always accepted the eccentricities of my orbit with extraordinary grace, we had never spoken much about them. Not until well after the book was published did I become a middle-aged man myself, and begin to see something of what my father must have seen in the time described in *What Becomes You*.

As a writer, I'm not the man I was, but I'm stuck with him—he wrote my book. Text stops time, fixing not only the moment described in the text, but also the moment at which you wrote it. The young writer I was spoke to the farce of having human power without authority, but was often ignorant of an equally incomprehensible farce, of having authority without power. My father understood a great deal about life that I did not at the time I wrote about him. I chose to make his character a minor one rather than risk a grossly inaccurate portrait, but the fact is that neither what I wrote nor anything I could have written at the time would have done him justice. The fact that text is fixed on publication may make our lives as writers more complicated, but it encourages us to keep learning and keep writing. I am now a middle-aged man who resembles my father, and I know more of what he knew. However, my ways of knowing the world now and the purposes to which I turn them as a writer are mine, not his, just as the story in which he appeared only as a minor character served my purposes, not his.

Unless I am in the business of journalism, ghostwriting, or technical writing, when I write, the purpose that takes priority is the writer's. Unlike my mother, my father wasn't responding to *What Becomes You* as the writer. His role brought up what, for me, is the biggest dilemma involved in writing nonfiction. As a human being, commitment to my craft seems like a lousy excuse to put my feelings and needs above those of the people I'm writing about—especially when these people are my family.

I'm a writer anyway. I've also been a zookeeper, a silversmith, and a day laborer. I understand making art as a job of work like any other, with its own occupational hazards. It contains whatever ordinary dignity comes from making the commitment to quit a job that isn't worth what it costs you, and if it is, to do your job well. The best description I've ever read of an artist's work is attributed to Robert Mitchum, who survived for years on a variety of odd jobs before becoming a movie star. When asked in an interview whether he liked acting, Mitchum is reported to have said, "It's better than breaking rocks." I think being a writer is better than breaking rocks, too.

When you've done the best work you can, what's left is the choice to show the work to others, or not, to make revisions based on their suggestions, or not, and to submit the work for publication, or not. I'm glad I went through this process with my brother and my father before *What Becomes You* was published, and I'm glad that the book was published. The process brought me closer to my brother's family, and my father's discomfort with what he read also unexpectedly brought us closer; it persuaded him to share more of himself and his life. Every year shortens the time we have left together, and I am grateful for what I have of him.

If family is the connecting link between private life and public history, then telling family stories means reimagining knowledge as the changing experiences of real people, rather than the universal pronouncements of abstract "experts." It means keeping our past alive while giving up the hope and the burden of being able to save any stories but your own. What we can tell is ours to tell. Everything we can't tell is someone else's story—someone who may or may not speak, and who may or may not agree with us. We can only leave space in our lives and work for these voices to be heard. At the end of the day I tell myself what I learned from my brother and my father, both lovers of music: that *rest* is the name for a particularly useful form of silence that comes between notes. Without the rest, music becomes an exercise in endurance. Without the music, there will be no rest.

My mother and I wrote a book together. In doing so, we had an unusual privilege; like all privileges, its advantages were inseparable from its challenges. We could write history and theory about gender roles, sex, and science in the United States from the 1950s to the present day. As a historian and philosopher of science (myself) and a professor of women's and gender studies (my mother), we both could use sex change as a lens through which to look at gender, sexuality, and culture over the past half century. Or we could write a book about my sex change—what it was like for me and for my mom. Being naturally contrary, we chose to do both. The most important decision we had to make was whether to write in personal or objective voices. The objective voice offers a level of personal shelter and a source of social authority that can be almost overwhelmingly attractive. However, when I was a kid in the 1970s, my mom taught me a feminist catchphrase I only began to really understand twenty years later: "The personal is political." It's true, not just for certain people but for all of us—as Patricia Hampl pointed out.

One of the most unexpected gifts of the personal voice has been the way that I could join my readers in laughing about things that I could only render in the objective voice in a tone of concealed outrage or misery. Not only did this process heal my own heart, it taught me that it is often more effective to deflate the world's evils than to declare war on them. And in my own case at least, it certainly makes for better prose. Another gift has been that by choosing to write—and to be a reader of my mother's writing—in the personal voice, I have discovered a parent as an equal, a colleague, a friend and a peer. We had to be willing to see each other in this way, not only as parent and child, but also as two similar and very different writers, human beings living out the same stages of our lives in different circumstances, bodies, and generations. It isn't easy to learn to see each other this clearly, especially for parents and children. No process in my life has been more rewarding.

In the personal voice, however, we both have to acknowledge ourselves not only to each other but also to readers: as writers, as observers, as laughing, angry, ironic, deadly serious, as the author of a reality on the page that comes from a particular perspective. First-person point of view requires me to say who I am and where I'm standing when I look into the world, find something I think is worth reporting, and speak of it to the reader. In investigating this perspective and its sources of understanding and authority, I have to be able to write about what I see and where I stand—and therefore the places and people that have shaped me—with both honesty and clarity. This is something that writing about personal material in the objective voice will not require you to do. I believe it is a vital task: for ourselves, our families, our cultures, our history, and any hope we have for a better future.

In the personal voice, we have to decide what to say about—and to—our parents, kids, cousins, friends, students, colleagues, partners, in various kinds of public forums. Then we have to experience the results of our choices.

The personal voice gives permission to see the writer as a human being, with a body, relatives, limited experience, and a point of view. In my case, for every time this permission has been misused by critics, theorists, or audiences, a dozen voices have offered me learned and extraordinary new family stories in the personal voice. These stories and their voices—because they dissolve ignorance, overturn assumptions; because they are unexpected, interesting, and true—are pure gold. They teach me what I did not know, and what I did not know I knew, instead of merely confirming my prejudices. The process gives me whatever wisdom I can claim—it teaches me how my stories may connect with other people's. As a writer, this is the most fertile ground I can imagine in which to grow good work. The family stories I am given in the personal voice reveal ways that everyday human stories become identified with each other and with our great myths. They reveal the seedy cores of scholars' and artists' brilliant insights. And they are often whispered into my ear after a reading, spoken hurriedly in a car on the way to the airport, slipped into my hand in a page of writing not for publication, please.

Judging by this evidence, when we write we are most often terrified of the stories that are ours to tell, and terrified most by the ones that are the most interesting. They are the stories powerful enough to shape our lives and our world, and they are often stories no one else has the power to tell. People offer these stories to me for safekeeping. But they are given to me rather than someone else precisely because I chose not to keep safe; I wrote, I showed up and told my stories—for publication, please.

I have said that I can tell no one's story but my own. Yet in my life and work, I am constantly being given other people's stories. In learning, unlearning, and revising them, I have discovered myself. Does this process make them mine? Does the fact that they were never mine to begin with leave me carrying a burden of stories I can't tell? What can I do with them?

It turns out this is the same question we've been struggling with all along, the question of how to write about your family.

So where does it all leave me at the end? What can I do with this damn essay on my desk?

I can do a few things with "Things We Don't Talk About." I can send it out anonymously. I can revise the story—as fiction, for instance—to change its circumstances or the way they're named. Or I can take a risk and trust my family as readers, because real-life stories can end well.

There's an additional choice we usually don't talk about. It's an option many writers sharing their stories with me have taken. Just tell the story—whatever story is in you, in whatever way you can tell it. Don't worry about who's helped or hurt by it, whether it's true with a capital T, current or safe or salable. Don't worry about who will see it. Whatever becomes of one particular version of a story, it matters to tell it.

The essay's still on my desk, where it may stay. But the only way to revise silence is to speak. Once you have written down a story—any story—you can change it. You can make a story evoked from your experience move more skillfully toward different ends. And if no one else in the world has told your stories for you, you get to do that job for yourself. Don't throw what you started with away. Just make a new space to revise, and revise, and revise. Because I wrote an essay about my family, I could write—and revise—a new one. I like the latest version. In it, I get to share the story called "Things We Don't Talk About" with my family. And I get to share it with you, a reader and writer, who can tell the story in a different way, with another ending.

You Can't Burn Everything

ALLISON HEDGE COKE

First draft. Sixth grade. Mrs. Minor's room.

Near the end of the spring semester, just before finals, I turned in a large ream of manuscript, handwritten, titled "The Diary of a Mad Housewife's Daughter" for extra credit to Mrs. Minor, our sixth-grade English teacher. She'd been so decent to me, never treating me as if I were different from anyone else in the room, something I'd rarely experienced at that time in my life. So I wanted to offer her something I'd shown no one else. I wanted to come clean with my own life with someone outside it.

The film *Diary of a Mad Housewife* had been released, rated M for mature, so no one under seventeen was allowed. Still, Mom was back in the asylum, getting shock treatments, and I knew her story and my own, so my mind was set to write the daughter's side of what I imagined the movie to be. I've never seen it—to this day—so I have no idea if it was about a schizophrenic who was acutely insane.

The weekend passed. I wondered what Mrs. Minor thought of it and how much she'd read. Returning on Monday, I was completely shocked to discover she'd worked out with the high school and local college to get me into advanced writing classes at their schools. My novel was groundbreaking, she said, and she wanted to help me.

Trouble is, it was memoir, and not affordable information for anyone outside the family to have.

I took the manuscript, ran home down the same alley and across the corner and up our block's alley as well, directly to the old coal stove we had in back for marshmallows and hot dogs, the stove my grandmother had used in the dugout they'd lived in. It was supposed to be a laundry stove, but they used it for everything back then: heat, cooking, you name it. My family used it for cookouts and fun, and a box of matches was just inside one of the lids on top toward the back near the chimney space.

As propelled as I had been to write the memoir, I was equally propelled now to burn it. I simply put the manuscript into the stove and then struck a match and let the fire consume it, my first full memoir draft and collective biography of my mother's insanity up to that point, a record of the systematic dismantling of our family and cultural, political, economic despair and glory, of our lives and the effect of her illness upon all of us, especially her.

It was done as quick as it had started. There was no way to explain to the well-intentioned Mrs. Minor, whom I completely respected and appreciated, that anyone who read it could return me to foster care, or worse. My mother finding out could cause who knows what. Anything was possible. The book was a totally unaffordable divulgence and it was not my right to make things hard on my mom, or dad, as he was responsible for her completely, or Mrs. Minor, for that matter. Least of all, for me. The truth of it could not be told because we were in the core of it and it was happening. The story was real, and anything could happen as a result of its release, so there could be no release. Certainly not anything my family could be hurt by, and I would have never shown it to any of them to read, the consequences heavily imagined by me and too much to bear.

Second draft. One-month residency-fellowship. MacDowell.

Out in a cabin on the MacDowell Colony, rustic enough at that time but lush enough to splay the muse, you didn't worry about anything but the work, and work came easy for a young writer who'd been given four weeks' reprieve from all distractions. I'd have a chance to knock out a full draft of a memoir I'd begun. Working with incarcerated juveniles and traumatized adults, I'd been struck by how few nonfiction texts existed that they could relate to or grow from. I imagined something in my own story might resonate.

I had come to MacDowell from a reservation, where my love was now buried. He'd died from leukemia nearly six years before, and I was having a dear time of it and letting go of nearness. I'd dated other people since; I was trying to move on, make the effort. Unfortunately, it wasn't taking, and I'd find myself at the cemetery reminiscing about his touch and just without much hope and wondering why people are so caught up on petty matters rather than matters of the heart and the work we do toward helping others in life, and just having a time of it.

The residency enriched and empowered me, providing the option of sleeping in the cabin/studio or a room in the rather stately guesthouse. The grounds offered a library, a performance space, a game room and dining room, an old amphitheater, lawns, natural ground under wooded canopy, and views of the White Mountains. Coming from a depressed reservation out on the savanna of the northern Plains, from a depressed life, widowed, unwanted, and unhealthy, with bouts of cancer lasting for eleven years already, I could catch up on some work without being criticized by neighbors for "trying to be a writer."

I was so broke that year, substitute-teaching and doing artists' residencies in schools, that I had to board my boys at St. Catherine's Indian School. They probably needed the break from me, since I'd returned to the same depression I was in just after Bill's death and wasn't in great shape. Their first month at school was my month at MacDowell, so the timing proved useful for all of us. Separated from all I was at the time and placed into some nice digs for the running, it was time to work, and revisiting the past became a soul-searching undertaking that would emit the full draft of my memoir in the works that became *Rock, Ghost, Willow, Deer*. I am indebted to Mac-Dowell.

In my time in the cabin, working on the memoir, each time I divulged something seriously baring, it became apparent to me that that particular remembered event wasn't the first time, or the only time, I'd experienced that element and that my seasons in life contained far more misses than hits—aside from punches, of which I'd received multitudes. The writing of it, the self-assessing and self-involvement, felt suicidal. Going there was wickedly rough. Each visualization opened doors to sure wounding, and knowing that my pain wasn't something anyone else on earth felt bad about was just killer. To clarify, I did not feel suicidal, but the work to get there, the process, felt like a suicide attempt. That's the deal. Knowing that the work, if published, would potentially open up issues that extended back to my early childhood—where whole communities are culpable when a child is suffering—was unnerving, to say the least. The walks and the cabin helped me to regain composure, and the beautiful surroundings were like cake, a bit of sweetness while doing necessary personal work.

Fortunately, having moved them to California to spare them more of my brother's violence, I'd already spent some time living near enough to my folks, in 1995 and 1996, that I'd been able to share parts of the chapter drafts with them. They'd had the chance to scrutinize my recollections. Most of my childhood had been blanked out of my mother's memory by shock treatments, so she checked sections that mentioned her own family or childhood, though she also read the entries I passed to my dad and older sister.

It was interesting. They'd become so impassioned about anything they remembered differently, or hadn't known about, or forgot, but the next day, they would suddenly provide me with details I may have been to young to know about, or had been excluded from. My dad did ask me to consider not writing it, for my mother's sake, as he felt it was upsetting her. My mother, on the other hand, was the only person who said it is what I did—write—and I always had, so this was just part of it.

During this process, both parents also shared stories of their own. My dad divulged to me that he'd written a play that had been produced and then plagiarized by his college professor, and my mother brought out short stories she'd written during World War II while working in

Ingles War Factory in Toronto as a young widow. In admitting their own endeavors, long put aside to get through the living we were put to, they were demonstrating the family propensity to write.

My sister kept telling me to write mysteries, because that is "what sells." She abhorred the idea of any of her friends reading my work about my own life and argued with my depictions of it, which, again, she had little knowledge of. Even as children we were not always in the same place. She'd leave for summer programs elsewhere, and I stayed with other families much more than she did.

Still, without that early family interaction, and giving the three of them opportunities to make any insertions of their own memories within the text at the time, I probably would not have been able to enter into the space I allowed for at MacDowell and get to the real work, that memory I'd repressed and there unfolded, the heart of the book. I left with a few hundred pages drafted. Getting to a place where I could write those recollections was agony, as so much of the full draft and expanded early chapters was memory I had withheld. No one had seen this draft, and I could barely deal with it. In fact, immediately following, I entered counseling for posttraumatic stress disorder and to begin deal with the understanding that, yes, repressed memory was an actual experience in long-term coping. Still, I wanted to be open and inclusive with the work at hand.

At this point, I told my dad about the original sixth-grade draft and my fear of its revelations and how I'd burned it to prevent anyone from doing anything to any of us, and he just looked so defeated that I felt guilty for revealing that as well. It was clear he'd wanted what was best for us all. He clearly understood my need to write it, though he also wished the need had not existed and blamed himself for it, albeit unnecessarily.

I highly recommend involving those whose mutual or conflicting memories might enhance the work with wider perspective. I do not recommend making drafts available to anyone who may wish you harm, whether they are in the memoir or not.

Rock, Ghost, Willow, Deer would not exist without my family's willingness to include what they would of their own memories in the early chapter drafts during this time. It would not exist without that time at MacDowell.

Proofs.

Several years later, when my revised memoir manuscript had been accepted by a publisher, the proofs came. I asked for them to be delivered to my folks' place and flew there to read through them with my eldest son and parents. I wanted to ensure that, despite their dismay at my having written the book, my family could tolerate its delicate inclusions. I also wanted it to be as accurate as possible, so I invited their input.

My son helped immensely with finding lines my editor had inserted that are things I just wouldn't say. He was also editorially essential in finding events that he and his brother were a part of and allowing me opportunity to excise or amend anything he felt either of them would suffer from.

My dad seemed both proud and somewhat put out by the whole thing, worried mostly about my mother and me, but generous as he always is, he tried not to show it, and suggested that I add that if we keep silent about abuse then we are also a part of it and that when we allow ourselves the ability to speak out, we are doing so for others as well.

My mother became very proud that the book was coming out and repeatedly stated that I was a writer, that this was what writers do, and that it was my life and of course I had to write it—in between taking time to tell off the Buggers in her bedroom. This part of the process is what worried my dad the most. He is, of course, protective of my mother and doesn't like any stress around her to set her off on delusional challenges.

My sister also continually called, mostly insisting I get rid of the manuscript and write mysteries.

The process was difficult, even still, but by now, they were realizing the book was happening, and we were coming to terms with our shared and secret lives. They also realized and appreciated that I had invited them into the process while in early stages of chapter work before the major draft. What they did not expect were the private revelations that I was divulging throughout the memoir, things they had not known. So this reading, with the four of us at the old gate-leg table, was the first time that allowed them into those portions of my life, and this proved difficult. Here is where they met my fates and found painful truths. My mother took it into her delusions and rocked it out of herself and then came and had coffee with me while she praised me for publishing, but my revelations proved more difficult for my father and oldest son. My dad kept apologizing for being "a terrible parent," which he was not, and thus I continually told him that he gave me every bit of the strength I'd had to get through it all, and none of it was his fault, and that the book, I hope, conveys this specifically. My son was just plain sickened by it all and really hates the painful contents of the book, overall, I think, but he is also a writer and a really fascinating one at that, and a terrific editor, too, so I enjoyed his willingness to go page by page and line by line through it.

I did not include my brother in this process, as we had not been in touch for years already. His actions had been so brutal that my editor had often cut them from the manuscript. His name is not in the book, nor would the press include family photos that included him. Yet he is a part of it and integral to everything related to my being the second daughter of the village crazy, as the onset of our mother's mental illness occurred at his birth, fifteen months after mine. He never had a chance, so to speak.

I do not recommend allowing a read-through to anyone who might wish you harm. And trust me, he definitely has meant me harm on more than a few occasions.

Shelf life. 2004 onward. South Dakota, New York, Michigan, New Mexico, Nebraska.

Since publication, I've been ridiculed by a few students who have taken deep issue with revealing family pain; by some friends, who really are not; by my daughter-in-law; by my sister (who would prefer to pretend that her version of my life is the true version); and by a couple of those guilty of the abuse the book records. One group of Native students, not affiliated by blood with anyone in my family at all, took issue with me "talking about your mother like that."

Yet my mother approved of it wholly, despite her battles with the Buggers, or maybe because of them, and my father had asserted our need not to protect abusers and to speak openly about taboo illnesses like schizophrenia. My oldest son was supportive, is glad it is out there, and wishes it had received more attention. My younger son's wife apparently used the material in the book as weaponry toward him and me, but then when people want artillery, they will find it.

Anyone who wants to do you harm will find ways to do it, so I recommend this not stopping you from doing the work you are propelled to do.

Culturally, the book is what our lives are. Nothing more, nothing less. Still, some readers looking to engage with what they expect from a Native memoir may not find what they expect, as the book is particular to my own mother's illness and its effects on our lives. Although our familial culture grounds us all throughout, the foundation of it, the function, is not sensationalized or commodified in the writing, so someone from outside might have other expectations that this book will not fulfill. Nor should it.

Such is the calamity of authorship and authenticity in revealing secrets. The work is what it is. The journey is what we are sharing, and the untold revelation is the seed of it all, the heart. This is what we offer, we who have ourselves to give in this way. The boundaries we tread upon in touching the taboo, the unsaid, and the deeply repressed are boundaries often in need of cultural healing and of change. Thus the memoirist.

Of course, this may open us up to ridicule, mockery, abuse, and even episodes of stalking, as happened to me. Who knows? It also opens doors for the author, for most of the readership, and for those family and friends who stick with the author to enjoy freer lives as a result and to move in new directions. Memoir is what we are, in some sense: a slice of us and a slice of the life. Not all-inclusive, not comprehensive, not autobiography, but a select account that fits within a sphere of wider life. The writing of memoir can prove extremely challenging (I underwent treatment for PTSD after writing the draft at MacDowell and again just before the book was released). Yet despite the disadvantages, I hope such texts will stay in print to help others in their own lives and reckonings, or simply to let them step into another person's footsteps for perspective.

You can't burn everything. Sometimes the story needs to be told.

Done with Grief

The Memoirist's Illusion

SANDRA SCOFIELD

My grandmother, Frieda Hambleton, died in 1983 in her house on Grant Street in Wichita Falls, Texas. A year later it burned to the ground. The house had been sold, but no one was living in it at the time. When my aunt called to tell me about the fire, I said, *Oh good.* She said, *I feel the same way.*

We didn't want the house, or mind if other people lived in it, but while it was standing, we kept thinking of her inside: rolling out biscuits in the kitchen, washing off the flour dust in the bathtub after work, putting fresh sheets on the bed.

I was relieved that a house in a city I had not set foot in since 1981 was no longer there to remind me of who had lived in it. I would never see Grant Street again. There was no chance I would be drawn to the house out of sentimentality or curiosity. Gone. There was something of the pyre about its destruction. It was her house, and as much as we still cried for her, we had to admit it had not been worth saving. There was something of exorcism, too. Maybe we could let go. Maybe we could slip from her grasp.

Thirty years later, I am still pondering that grasp, and sorting the ways my grandmother shaped my family and my life.

My aunt sent me two boxes from the house. She told me they held an old Bible, letters, photographs, my grandmother's baptism certificate, a few other documents. I remember how slowly I unwrapped the boxes, how I found a place for them in the bottom of our kitchen pantry, how I told myself I would look at everything as soon as I could.

It was many years before I examined their contents. I dreaded the surge of melancholy I knew would fill me. I was waiting until I felt better, but when I pulled the boxes out, it was because I felt compelled: called, if you will, by letters brittle with age, and black and white photographs, and social security cards, and poems copied by my grandmother into her Bible—sentimental verses meant to calm a grieving heart.

I was right to fear unpacking, of course, and the grief that coursed through me made my body heavy, made me almost mute. Thoughts of my mother, who had died in 1959, tormented my sleepless nights, too. I couldn't have said what hurt most. All I could think to do was write. I had written novels, stories, poems, and book reviews; I had written since I was a small child; surely I could write about my family. I thought it would be like breaking a blister, painful but healing.

I wanted to be done with childhood. I wanted to be done with grief.

I soon learned that I could not write about everything at once. After almost a year of false starts, I decided to focus on my mother and me, to try to tell how a child takes everything into her heart and into her body, too, and how love and God and sex get all mixed up when you are trying to be like your mother before you know her, or yourself, well enough to understand what that would mean. My memories of my grandmother contracted to what was relevant to the story in front of me. For two years I thought about my mother every day and about the work of the manuscript, but when I finished, thoughts of Frieda were still there, like a radio in the room. I missed her; if ever there was unconditional love, it was what she gave me. Though I had grown up in her home, Frieda had never told me what to do; she had never criticized me or refused me refuge or small handouts. She had lived to see me have a daughter and a good marriage, but as I thought about her, I still felt like her child. I wanted to press one more time against the cool cushion of her chest.

I thought if I wrote about Frieda, I could replace the rest of my roiling sorrow with stable memories. Writing about my grandmother would not be complicated. There was no unfinished business, no mystery. I thought I knew what to say before I began. The story was so simple:

Once there was a woman who loved her granddaughter without reservation.

That was the story I knew about the woman I called "Mommy." It had no dark alleys. It was just Frieda and me. Mostly me.

I have been at it for years now. I should have known better.

Before I started writing about my mother, I asked myself what the point was. With exorcism of the past at one end of the spectrum, and enshrinement at the other, I couldn't predict a likely landing place. I didn't want to lose my connection to the dead, but I didn't want to make myself sick with questions that had no answers. What I wanted was to be at peace with my sorrow. I have a deep belief in the power of craft, and I thought that if I could get past the rush of remembering, memory would become an object I could turn about for better perspectives.

I wasn't all wrong. I expected to feel bad at first, and I did: angry, resentful, sad, lonely, confused, frustrated. I just kept writing, pushing through. Like any other draft, my first version of the story was unfocused and ill proportioned. It wasn't really the story at all. But with something down on paper, I could start chipping out the narrative and building it into something cohesive. I could climb out of all the feelings into work.

What I hadn't figured on was the way that processing memory settles it. Mother standing in the window—a flitting, fragmentary, painful but cherished recollection—became a woman on a page, and I stopped "seeing" her at all. In a very real sense, my book put her on the shelf. Maybe I thought I could do that trick again with Frieda, but so far, I'm not even close.

I started writing about my grandmother to quiet the noises in my head. *Remember and be done with it* was the mantra. But I did have questions. I wondered why she would never talk to me about my mother after her death; why she never once mentioned her husband, Ira, who died when she was thirty, leaving her with three small children. Why she always said things like, "It's not up to me," or "There's no use in talking about it," and yet others in the family were so often mad at her, sometimes stomping out of the house, slamming the door. I wondered what she had thought all those times she didn't criticize me, the times when I was foolish and selfish; I cringed to think of what must have been in her mind.

She was an angry person (thin lips, chin up, shoulders tight, hard steps walking away) but a fiercely loyal matriarch, withholding of what she was thinking and feeling but generous with what she thought you needed. She was suspicious and she made me think I couldn't trust anyone except family, when you could tell she thought everyone in the family did wrong things without even trying. But a lot of the time she was the only one I had, and I knew she loved me.

I discovered things that shocked me—a couple extra husbands in there—and I got a deeper understanding of the grief that fed her anger—a lot of people died young. Most surprising of all, I began to see what I had learned from her, what we all lost to grief, the ways I am like her. My tendency toward suspicion, resentment, huffy resignation. My tight hold on my special sorrows. I've sat on it all a while now, and I can see I have two big tasks: to stop judging her, and to stop being her. I still don't know if I can do that best by telling or by silence.

You think: I'll show what life was like for us, for me, for them. I can do that, at least. An homage of sorts, a sign of respect.

You think: I'll sort out myth and truth and be honest and unflinching.

You think: I'll find a pattern, a reason, something to take away as the reward for all the work.

But you just don't know what you will find. A Pandora's box. A virus. A party line. A tribunal. A hole with no bottom. I don't think writing will close the box, or fill the hole, anymore. Pick up, put down; that's the rhythm of months, now years. There is mystery, because life is mysterious, all life, all persons. I can't solve it and I can't forget it. I can't make a plot or an argument out of memory and mystery. All I can do is scrabble. I went over a mountain, that's all. It's behind me now, but I'm in the shadow. I opened the boxes, and they won't be closed again.

4
Conversations
of Hope

The Seed Book

STEPHANIE ELIZONDO GRIEST

Write as though your parents are dead.

I have been instructing my students to do this for nearly a decade now, yet I have never actually done so myself. For starters, if my parents actually *were* dead, I wouldn't be writing at all. I would be strapped to a gurney in a psychiatric unit, mumbling at the ceiling.

I wish I were kidding . . . but I'm not. I am one of those rare writers who absolutely adores her parents. How could I not? When I decided, at age twenty-four, to quit my perfectly respectable job with health insurance and a 401K to write my first memoir (about a four-year romp through Russia, China, and Cuba), they let me move back in with them. For a year. Not only that, but Mom read and edited every page of every draft I wrote. Dad, meanwhile, brought me home a Subway sandwich every day for lunch and cooked me dinner. The book that finally hit store shelves was just as much their creation as my own. Dad, a Rush Limbaugh–loving Republican, even monogrammed his favorite shirt and baseball cap with the book's title, *Around the Bloc*, accompanied by a communist red star.

So I would rather pirouette off a bridge than hurt my parents in any way. They, in turn, would rather pirouette off a bridge than obstruct my career. The only time Mom has ever asked me to change anything I've written is when she fears it makes *me* look bad. For my first memoir, that meant whittling down the recounting of a disastrous relationship with an emerald-smuggling Colombian I met in college and chased around the globe for three years.

"It makes you sound desperate," she said.

It did. I was. Out it went.

When it came to the section about her own family, however, Mom not only didn't balk, she helped me iron out the details. Even the painful ones—like the afternoon her own mother tucked her and her four brothers and sisters into the bed they shared, an old mattress on a hardwood floor, and then walked into her bedroom, locking the door behind her. A blast rang out moments later. The eldest sister pounded on the door and, when she heard no response, gathered her siblings and herded them next door, where their *tía* and *tío* lived. The siblings were soon split up among their mother's family, while their father remarried and had seven more kids. Tía and Tío, who had no children of their own, inherited Mom and two of her brothers and later took in the twins a neighbor down the street had abandoned.

Growing up, I knew nothing of this story. Tía and Tío were my grandparents, plain and simple. But I started suspecting otherwise in my seventh-grade Spanish class, when I learned that *tía* and *tío* mean aunt and uncle—not grandma and grandpa. I started snooping around my parent's drawers for answers and eventually found a death certificate tucked inside a yellowing envelope. The name up top—Barbara Silva Elizondo—seemed significant, as Barbara is my sister's name and Elizondo is my mother's maiden name. Yet this woman died in 1949, at age twenty-five. Who could she be? I read until the end, where something swept a chill through my veins. Under cause of death, it said gunshot wound to the head.

This document haunted me for a decade, but I never asked about it until Mom visited me while I was living in Beijing. It was the first time we had ever spent so much time together, just the two of us, and being so many thousands of miles from home dissolved every barrier between us. We talked more candidly than ever before, and one afternoon, while sharing a picnic on the grounds of the Summer Palace, I asked about that death certificate.

"It's my mother's," she said, taking a swig of orange juice.

"But . . . it said she died of a gunshot wound."

"She killed herself," she said, capping the bottle.

"Why?" I breathed.

"She had five kids before she turned twenty-five. That's reason enough."

Years later, when I tried to recast this moment into prose, Mom sifted through my manuscript pages and helped me get it right. Not just the facts of her mother's suicide, but the theories. Some said she killed herself because she was depressed. Or because she was pregnant again. Or because the father of her next child was not her husband. Or because her husband was unfaithful. Her own mother insisted that she didn't kill herself at all, but that someone must have slipped into her bedroom and shot her. But police didn't fully investigate homicides back then—not those of impoverished Mexican women, anyway. Even when they left no note and said no good-byes.

If this memory excavation upset my mother, she didn't show it. And I didn't ask, for ambition had consumed me. All I could think about was finishing—and selling—that book, which took half a decade. The ramifications of writing our history didn't occur to me until *Around the Bloc* was finally published in 2004 and I went on tour. At one of my first events, I read aloud the passage about that picnic in Beijing. Afterward, a man standing in my book line requested a signature. When I asked his name, he replied, "I'm the son of one of those twins who got abandoned down the street."

I looked up to find a cousin I had never known. Remarkably, he wasn't angered by the callous way I had portrayed his origins. He seemed almost grateful, as though the story legitimized what his family had endured. We fell into each other's arms, startled by the bonds of history.

This scene repeated itself as I traveled around the country, most memorably at the Barnes and Noble in my hometown, Corpus Christi, Texas, where a hundred people gathered, a quarter of them family. When I reached the passage where my grandmother tucked in her children for the final time, a golf ball lodged inside my throat. I peeked up from the book, half expecting to duck a soaring shoe. But no. My mother and her brothers were nodding in unison. The silence that had shrouded their tragedy for half a century was about to shatter, and they gave me permission to do so.

Afterward, we gathered in my parents' backyard for cake and margaritas. Family gatherings were often angst inducing, as everyone anywhere near my age was procreating. They balanced plump babies on their hips. Even my "little" cousins had couches and houses and spouses, while I slept on a futon in the Brooklyn apartment I shared with multiple roommates. Though I was pushing thirty, I felt embarrassingly adolescent in their presence.

But that evening, they cornered me one by one, as though my book possessed the same magnetic lure as their babies. "Is it true?" they asked. "Did that really happen to us?"

I should interject here the other major source of angst in my life then: cultural identity. Mom faced so much ridicule for her Spanish accent during her own childhood, she decided not to pass it on to my sister or me. Despite growing up only a hundred and fifty miles from the Mexico border, I could barely say *baño*. I don't look especially Mexican either: my skin is light and my eyes are blue, courtesy of Dad's Pennsylvania Dutch genes. Yet nearly every accolade I had ever received—from minority-based scholarships to my book contract— could be attributed to my Mexican heritage, a fact that induced as much guilt as gratitude. Ever since college, I had been trying to Mexify myself, building shrines to the Virgen de Guadalupe, supporting Latino arts and causes, and drinking rounds of margaritas.

That evening in my parents' backyard, however, I found a new way of fitting into my family. From that point on, I was the chronicler of our history. Family trees, photographs, newspaper clippings, and memories began trickling down to me. People started telling me things they had never told each other. "Now don't you go writing about this, *mija*," they'd say, but with a wink that meant I should.

Emboldened by this experience, I commenced a new memoir project—this time, about origins. What had our family lost during our migration from Mexico? After a full-immersion Spanish course, I set off for our motherland. For months I scoured the countryside, searching for something familial—a name, a place, a face. Once I'd tracked down my grandmother's ancestral village in the state of Tamaulipas, I invited Mom to join me. A plane, two buses, and a harrowing taxi ride later, we were standing in a plaza, surrounded by possible kin. We interrogated everyone who crossed our path, from shop owners to municipal officials to the region's eldest resident, but no one could recall a single Silva. Our pilgrimage concluded at a cemetery, where we wandered among the headstones. The oldest were difficult to read, their engravings worn smooth by rain. Yet I scrutinized each one. Badly hoping it would legitimize my connection to that nation, that people, that place. Badly wanting ancestors to anchor me. But while we made out headstones marked Pérez and Garcia, Garza and De León, none said Silva.

In the end, I left Mexico with only a story—yet one that birthed my second memoir, *Mexican Enough*. And that book charts the origins I *did* discover during the eight-month journey. Like road songs. Recipes. Tequila games. Poems. Prayers. I documented where our family's fortitude comes from—and our humility. Our predisposition to wrapping our furniture in plastic and decking our walls with icons. Our inability to sit still if music surges through a speaker. And language, language, language. Though I found no remnant of my grandmother in Mexico, I at least recovered her tongue. Linguistic peace at last.

My womb is empty as I write these words. Indeed, it has yet to house a tenant—and I recently turned thirty-seven years old. As I near the end of my childbearing years, I realize that books might be my only legacy. Rather than propagating the seeds of my ancestors, I'll be spreading their stories. In that sense, maybe I *do* write as though my parents are dead, as if *all* of us are dead. And memoir is the best way I know of perpetuating us.

Calling Back

LORRAINE M. LÓPEZ

My daughter, Marie, is gifted, impulsive, and scary. As she lurches toward thirty, her teenage years are still too traumatic for me to recall without doubling over, reaching for a chair. Once during this time, when she had the habit of climbing out her bedroom window to roam dark and empty streets, she was arrested for assaulting a police officer who accosted her at a phone booth after two a.m. on a week night. He asked her what she was doing out this late. Her response was to bite him. Her probation officer, Kim, arranged for us to meet with the police officer and work out an agreement in order to avoid jail time for my daughter. The police officer, a blushing redhead, entered the meeting so timorously that I knew he had no more business upholding the law than I have manning a space shuttle. When Kim asked him if he had anything to say to Marie, he stammered, "I just want to know why you bit me." Marie shrugged and said he shouldn't have bothered her while she was on the phone. I nudged her to be more contrite, but I thought, *Of course. Anyone knows better than that.* Though not a violent woman, I suppressed the impulse to bite him myself, then and there. In this moment, I grasped my daughter, this urge, the flash of rage this feeble officer ignited. I abandoned myself and whooshed into her life—where things were happening, real things, hard things—just for this instant, an instant I call back again and again by writing about her.

My daughter and I are well matched. I am a compulsive writer and she is an addictive, even obsessive reader even from her early years.

She was the kind of child who would stumble into pillars and walls obscured by the book in front of her face. Like a chain-smoker, she scarcely finishes one novel before snatching up another. To feed her habit, I scour bookstores, yard sales, and libraries. Now that she is unhappily married, I send her novels about women who rise like phoenixes from the ashes of disappointing relationships. I have also written hard stories inspired by her, by her life. She reads these avidly, and still she always wants more. Tell me, she seems to be saying, tell me how you see me, tell me what it is to be me. Call me back and tell me about me.

One morning not too long ago, I received an unsigned e-mail with normal capitalization, except that the sender consistently presented the personal pronoun "I" in lower case. The message read as follows:

i disagree that your characters are fiction, i read the story Soy la Avon Lady The character is based on your cousin who is the diva from LA, and your relatives who reside in New Mexico! Just be honest!

Typing this now, I realize how difficult it is to commit capitalization mistakes using most word-processing programs. My e-mail program likewise corrects such gaffes, especially when it comes to the first person singular "I," an error that I have come to associate—in my long experience of dealing with electronic messages from students and colleagues—with a phenomenally oversized ego. *My ego is so distended*, the lowercase "i" says to me, *that I should be famous like e. e. cummings.*

The message surprised me more than the capitalization. Who is this person who takes it upon herself (though unsigned, the e-mail address presented a distinctly female name) to exhort me—a fiction writer—to be honest? What is she saying? That I am not a fiction writer because she thinks she knows the people upon whom I have based some characters? And how can she claim to know them, if she refers to my aging cousin Molly, an itinerant Avon salesperson and temporary clerk-typist living in a tiny apartment with two geriatric cats, as a diva? And to whom shall I be honest to satisfy this disgruntled reader? Future interviewers? Myself? Shall I confess myself to her?

My first impulse was to answer the message. To ask the sender why she was writing me and what she wanted. But my delete finger, a cool and decisive pointer, acted swiftly and wisely. Not before I printed the message for my notes file, thinking, *Hmm, maybe someday I can use this.*

I complained about this message to my younger sister Frances, a family member who feels I don't write about her often enough, though she has given me the goods on extended family members so frequently that she should receive a cut of my royalties. Frances was livid about this attack on "our work." "Just send me that bitch's e-mail," she told me. "Just forward it to me. I'll kick her ass electronically."

I told her I'd deleted the message, not mentioning my dark secret, an obsession to save and file anything that provokes, irritates, interests, challenges, disrupts, amuses, hurts, or inspires me, so I can sort it all out and maybe settle a few scores by writing about it later. Small wonder I am drawn to write about family.

When I wrote my first book, I drew inspiration for many of the characters from my immediate and extended family. It's somewhat true that I believed the work would never be published, but it is also true that I was lazy and foolish, so I named names and hinted at particular and specific events in backstory. The main trajectories of my narratives are always imagined, but some characters are representations of family members. Here, I must add that I have always lived some distance from central New Mexico, where most of my extended family resides, so I usually learn about these relatives and events through gossip from willing informants like Frances and my other sisters. Something in these third- and fourth-hand accounts invariably sparks ideas for me. Gossip by definition is worth repeating. It usually has a natural narrative shape, attractive conflict patterns, and characters whose motives are curious, but clear. When these pragmatic considerations were combined with my desire to know more about the people to whom I am related, I couldn't resist the impulse to write about family.

It seems obvious to me now, but at the time, I never imagined my cousin Molly would take issue with being compared in appearance to an unconvincing transvestite. I couldn't fathom that another cousin, Geraldine, might resent my portrayal of her alcoholic brother and sexually confused son. And who knew that the oldest of my cousins, Barbara, would be so taken with her characterization as a psychotropic drug-addled loony that after reading the book she'd need to phone me often to sort through the circumstances contributing to her condition, as if I were a therapist?

Though I sent my stories out to journals on a regular basis and I collected them to submit for a literary competition, I must have kicked the rationalizations into overdrive or compartmentalized like crazy to disconnect these actions so determinedly from their consequences. Or my doubts the work would be published worked themselves into a strong conviction. Then, I suppose, when I won the prize and publication, I assured myself that no one would bother to read my book. And, if a few family members did pick up a copy and recognize themselves in my writing, well, aren't familial bonds unconditional? Of course, everyone would love and accept me just the same as always. I was wrong, wrong, and wrong.

Members of my immediate and extended family read my book almost as soon as it came out, and when I gave a reading in Albuquerque, I was astonished by the number of cousins, aunts, and uncles in attendance and how their faces were luminous with pride. They all had copies of my book—dog-eared and much thumbed through—for me to sign. My cousin Elsie was thrilled that I'd written about the white shoes she'd tossed into a fireplace in a bar on the night before her wedding, after she and her husband chucked in their champagne flutes and wanted to prolong the drunken celebratory moment. Another cousin, Clarence, was eager to know if he had been depicted as the aforementioned sexually confused youth, and he was crushed when I said, "No, that's not you. You're tossing cashews into your mouth in 'When Dad Shot Jesus.'" Cousins Dolores and Yolanda wanted to know why I hadn't written about them, and my youngest cousin, Juanita, regarded me in silence for a long while before asking, "All along, were you thinking like *that*? Were you thinking like a writer?" After my reading that night, my family took me to a bakery to celebrate. They prevailed on me to read another excerpt.

Neither Molly nor Geraldine attended.

Criticizing a film in *The New Yorker*, David Denby mentions that one character is a writer with the habit of dropping incidents from her family's life into her fiction. Denby writes: "But there is no way of telling whether [this character] is a good writer or a bad one, or whether she has made creative use of her family or merely exploited it." By this rubric, talent determines whether the writer uses family as inspiration or for exploitation. But there's something about the word "use" that sets my teeth on edge. How does a writer determine whether her work is sufficiently well-executed that family members shouldn't feel abused by recognizing their lives in it? Molly and Geraldine might point out that no matter how well the fiction is written, a family member is exploited when she feels exploited by it.

That night in the bakery I asked Clarence about Molly and Geraldine, their hard feelings, and he quipped, "Yeah, well, that's what happens when you write *friction*."

Months later, I did hear from Geraldine. She called me in Nashville and hung up on me. Twice. "How could you?" she kept saying. "How could you?" I told her that I thought I'd written a love story in writing about her family, a story about the enormousness of a father's love and forgiveness. "It's not a love story," she said. "It's a *hate* story." After she slammed down the phone for the second time, I never heard from her again. Every now and again, I think of her, and I ask my husband, "Do you think Geraldine has forgiven me yet?" He shakes his head and tells me to give her a bit more time.

After a couple of years, I was stunned to learn via the family grapevine that Molly no longer hated me. I didn't know she hated me to begin with, so this came as both a shock and a relief. At a family reunion, I spotted her looming in a nightclub where we had gathered to hear our cousin Concha's son and his wife perform music. Without thinking, I rose from my seat and crossed the room to embrace her. She hugged me back. "I can't be mad at you anymore," she said. "I was angry for a long time, and then I started writing." Molly pulled a sheaf of papers from her oversized handbag. "I always wanted to write, and you made me want to tell my side." I read her stories, and they are real and moving. But in them, she implicates her sister Barbara as culpable in the car accident that killed our grandmother, the wreck that unraveled my eldest cousin's mind.

"What do you think?" Molly wanted to know the next day.

"These are very powerful," I said before sharing the nugget of wisdom I had unearthed from my experience. "But don't show them to Barbara."

"Oh, I know," said my cousin Molly. "I never would."

Though the next day, during the talent show portion of the family reunion, Molly stepped up to the microphone and read her "stories" to a stunned audience of aunts, uncles, cousins, and her sister Barbara, who was seated up front, unflinching through all of it. When Molly finished, Barbara lunged from her seat, pounding her palms together: a standing ovation.

These days, Barbara continues phoning me, sometimes late at night, to discuss her childhood—the neglect she experienced—during uninterruptible monologues that stretch on for hours. Feeling like a trespasser who has been caught and is being held in a windowless place of stultifying dullness until the authorities arrive, I have listened and listened. Once after I was already in bed and drifting toward sleep, the phone rang and my husband answered it. "Barbara, how are you?" he said. I sprang from bed, waving my arms wildly in the universally recognized semaphore code for *I am* NOT *home*. He told her that she had just missed me and stayed on the phone for over thirty minutes as she poured out her troubles. After he finally managed to say good night and hang up, he sighed. "If you're going to keep writing about family," he said, "we seriously need to get caller ID."

When I realized that, contrary to my expectations, my first book would be published, I wanted to add a disclaimer that read: "All of the characters and events in this book are fictionalized. However, if you recognize yourself in these pages and are disturbed by what you read, you might want to make some changes." My publisher, a kind and wise man, dissuaded me from doing this. And he was right. What I mean to say is this: I cannot write a human being. I cannot create a life on paper, but I can write a fictional character who may share some traits and experiences with the people I know and love—often family members. And I usually model characters after complex people who intrigue and inspire me, those who capture my imagination through their depth, complexity, generosity of spirit, or humor. But mainly, I am drawn to write about the people I am curious about, those I have to call back—like Barbara—again and again, late at night and when I am alone, not just for the pleasure of their company, but because I want to know them better, to understand them and to understand myself better.

Like Rain on Dust

RICHARD HOFFMAN

I'm back in Pennsylvania at my father's kitchen table where the opening scene of my memoir, *Half the House*, takes place. My publisher's lawyers want signed releases from the people portrayed in the book.

"What is this you want me to sign?" asks my aunt Kitty. She holds the paper up by one corner as if it were wet and dripping.

"It's my publisher's lawyers." I know I've already explained this on the phone; that's why she's walked over here from her house. "They want to be sure you won't sue me."

"Sue you?" She makes a sour face, shakes her eighty-year-old head. "It's a book! If I don't like what it says, I can close it!" Then she reaches over and puts her hand on mine, squeezes, and adds, "Besides, I'm still your aunt Kitty, and if I don't like what you say about me in that there book, I'll come up to Boston and box your goddamn ears for you!"

The week before, I'd received a letter from Harcourt Brace's lawyers with a list of names of certain persons mentioned in my memoir from whom I would have to get releases. They included my father, my brother Joseph, my aunt, and the coach who had raped me when I was ten years old. The publication date was about a month away.

Half the House begins not with the usual disclaimer one finds in the front of novels, but with what might be called a reclaimer, since it was my purpose to reclaim all manner of lost things in its narrative. It spells out the kind of not-fiction it is and sets forth the rules I followed: "This is not a work of fiction. It contains no composite characters, no invented scenes. I have, in most instances, altered the names of persons outside my family. In one instance, on principle, I have not." Of course, that one instance was the coach. I left for Pennsylvania with the releases in hand. I made them up—three options and a place for a signature:

> I have read the manuscript of Richard Hoffman's memoir, *Half the House*, and I have no objection to its publication.
> I have been given the opportunity to read the manuscript of Richard Hoffman's memoir, *Half the House*, and I have declined. Nevertheless, I have no objection to its publication.
> I do not consent to the use of my name or other identifying characteristics in Richard Hoffman's memoir, *Half the House*.

My brother had read an earlier draft of the manuscript and was helpful in setting me straight about a few dates and other details I'd gotten wrong. He checked the first box and signed. My father and my aunt didn't want to read it and checked the second box, my father saying, "You and I have been through a lot together. We each have our own memories and our own way of thinking about them. I hope you sell a million copies of the book, but I don't think I want to read it."

I was not going to be able to ask the coach, Tom Feifel, to sign such a document, no way, no how, even if he was alive. I knew, however, that he had been arrested twice before for molesting young boys, so I went to the local newspaper looking for records, hoping that would satisfy the publisher's lawyers that Feifel had, indeed, done the kinds of things my book claimed. There was a file with his name on it, but whatever had been in there had been removed. I resigned myself to looking for records at the public library the next day, and if I failed, the courthouse.

When I got back to the house, my father handed me a piece of paper with a couple of phone numbers on it. Both were men he knew who had coached with Feifel. "Why don't you try calling these guys and see what they know?"

The first call was all I needed. I was able to get the year of one of Feifel's prior arrests, along with the name of the arresting officer. I called him as well. Although retired, he remembered the case well. Both men were angry that Feifel had been sentenced to probation and were willing to put their recollections in writing. The retired officer agreed to send me a copy of the police report. Both believed that Feifel had since died.

It was enough to allow the book to go forward, as long as I was willing to amend the contract to indemnify Harcourt Brace.

My father was right; we'd been through a lot together, and much of it was dramatized in the memoir. I'd taken great pains to portray him with enough complexity to at least suggest how complicated a man he was, how much suffering he shouldered, how inadequate the resources he had at his disposal, how humanly imperfect a father he had been, and what a mix of rage and love I bore toward him. But the book-jacket copy that came with the galleys was awful. It turned him into a cartoon: a cigar-chomping, hard-drinking World War II vet who beat his kids. My father was a paratrooper in the Second World War. He smoked cigars. He beat us. But he also worked, much of his life as a laborer, to try to keep us fed, often with two full-time jobs to make ends meet. Two of his four sons, my brothers Mike and Bob, were in wheelchairs and would die of Duchenne's Muscular Dystrophy. I had written about his lying to get away for a half hour from one job or another, coming home to lift my brothers into their beds when they'd become too heavy for my mother, about his long discourses on how the world worked and the importance of maintaining your dignity and decency, about his boyish love of sports, especially baseball. The book was dedicated to him. While my portrayal was an attempt to understand the man I loved most in the world, the first thing readers would be presented with was a caricature. I asked for and was given permission to rewrite the jacket copy.

During the many years of writing *Half the House*, I allowed my fear of my father's shame to impede my progress again and again. Sometimes I even worried that my father would read the book, be overwhelmed by it, and have a heart attack. Now I see that fear as so much self-importance. My father grew up with nothing during the Great Depression. He jumped from airplanes in the dark into machine-gun fire in the Second World War. And I thought that a book about our family would kill him?

I had tried in the months before publication to reassure him that the memoir was not a "hatchet-job." I reminded him that the book was dedicated to him. I told him that in my eyes his struggle, and my mother's, to cope with my brothers' illnesses and deaths, the lack of money, the lack of any help or even understanding from others outside the family, was the core of the book. "People who have read the manuscript consider you a heroic figure," I said. On the one hand, I knew I was soft-pedaling the book's content; on the other, I felt no need to remind him of other elements I feared he would fix on. I knew very well my father's capacity for shame and self-blame, and though I'd refused to be bound by it as a writer, I did not want to be the instrument of further suffering. I kept a slip of paper with a quote from Jung above my writing desk: "To show a person his darkness is to remind him of his light." I hoped it was true.

My aunt Kitty was the first to read the published book, and she wrote me a letter. Usually I open my mail standing at the kitchen table, the trash nearby for the credit card offers, the junk mail, the subscription requests, but I took her letter upstairs to my study and closed the door. I'd never had a letter from her before so I knew what it was. She wrote that she'd stayed up all night reading and what a gift it was to have "all these memories, all these reminders of things I'd forgotten. And there you were, all through those years, taking it all in, and remembering it all this time."

My father called a week later. "Well, you've got a big fan down here in Allentown!" he said.

"You mean Aunt Kitty. Yeah. She wrote me a beautiful letter about the book."

There was a long silence; just when I was about to say something, anything, to break it, he said, "Yeah. Well I read your book too."

Oh, shit. Another silence ticked by. "And?"

"And it's a good book. I might argue with you about a few things like whether something happened in the summer or the winter, or one year or the next, but it gives a pretty accurate picture of our family life during that period of time." He blew air into the receiver. "I'm proud of you," he added. Then he hung up.

A memoir is not what happened, it is a re-presentation of what happened. The hyphen I've placed in that word represents all the literary skill and all the honesty and judgment that goes into writing a truthful book. As philosopher Alfred Korzybski remarked, "the map is not the territory."

One day about six weeks after publication, my father called me.

"The son of a bitch is back," was all he said at first.

"What do you mean?"

"Feifel. The god-damned snake. He's back. Coaching."

"Where?"

"Right here in Allentown! It don't look like he ever really stopped. They're going to pick him up tomorrow. They've got new charges on him, new kids, ten, eleven years old. Some of the mothers got hold of your book. They're going to nail the son of a bitch this time."

"This is unbelievable."

"It's true. Talk to your brother Joe sometime. He was in a bookstore the other day and some woman come in and walked right up to the cashier, no browsing around or nothing, and asked the guy for your book. Joe says she was whispering and looking around to see if anyone was watching, and she stuck it in her purse like it was pornography or something and ran right out. When he told me, I says, 'I'll bet that was one of the mothers.' Anyway, I talked to a buddy of mine who says they got a warrant. They're going to slap the cuffs on him tomorrow or the next day."

What I didn't know yet, because he hadn't told me, was that my father was the one who had put the book in the hands of a friend of his who headed the youth organization where Feifel was coaching. My father's friend had spoken to the mothers of several boys who were often seen with him. One of them, it was true, was the woman my brother saw in the bookstore. But it was, in fact, my father who had set events in motion.

When I learned this, a few days later, I thanked him.

"I couldn't help it," he said to me on the phone. "I thought about these kids here. And I thought . . . I thought, what if you hadn't moved away? If you'd stayed in Allentown, then maybe my grandson, maybe Robert, would have been on that team, and I thought, hell, does this snake get a crack at the next generation too?"

I was crying by then, leaning on the counter in the kitchen of my house in Massachusetts.

"Man, I feel great!" my father was saying. "I feel fifty years younger!"

I have written elsewhere about the events that unfolded then: Feifel's trial and conviction, my father and I attending; the fact that more than four hundred men came forward to say they had been assaulted by Feifel when they were boys; the phone calls from all over the country, the letters from all over the world, the stories of men raped as boys by coaches, teachers, priests; Feifel's death in prison, a probable murder victim. I include all this here, in this essay, because it's important to point out that the impact of the memoirist's work goes beyond the reactions of family members. The trouble with the view put forth in dozens of books about family "dysfunction," some of them interesting and helpful, is that it tries to understand the family without its community, without its culture and class, without its history and the relation of that history to—well, History.

The aftermath of the book's publication changed my relationship to my father immensely. Instead of the occasional phone call about the Red Sox or the Phillies or a report on one of his young grandchildren's latest milestones, we became close. We talked about my mother, who had died in 1985, and about my brothers' short lives. We visited often, laughed and sometimes cried together. His new openness made him a wonderful grandfather to both of my kids who mourned him when he passed away in 2008.

But there is more to be considered than the personal, familial, or literary consequences of a work of nonfiction. Teaching a memoir workshop for a dozen years now, I have seen my students struggle with some of the same fears that plagued the writing of *Half the House*, chief among them being whether or not certain family members might feel hurt. During this same period, resistance to the genre has become a backlash, even a preemptive sneer. Articles in the *New York Times*, *Washington Post*, *Boston Globe*, and elsewhere all seemed to agree that memoir is a third-rate genre, peopled by unseemly victims licking their wounds in public.

On behalf of my students and to answer that public charge, I wrote this poem:

Messengers

> The house itself, if it had a voice
> Would speak out clearly. As for me,
> I speak to those who understand;
> if they fail, memories are nothing.
>
> AESCHYLUS, *Agamemnon*

We say what we know because we must.
You can cheer us or run us out of town.
It's nothing at first, like rain on dust,

a hairline crack in the faultline's crust,
a tentative first-person plural pronoun.
We say what we know because we must

recall, recount, redeem, and readjust
all that we've known, not for renown.
It's nothing at first, like rain on dust,

or the first few tiny flecks of rust
on barrels buried underground.
We say what we know because we must

talk back to histories we do not trust,
relearn our own, and set them down.

It's nothing at first, like rain on dust.

What does it mean to fear what's just?
You can cheer us or run us out of town.
We say what we know because we must.
It's nothing at first, like rain on dust.

The Bad Asian Daughter

BICH MINH NGUYEN

In the community of Vietnamese Americans in Michigan, where I grew up in the 1980s, good Asian daughters become dentists or pharmacists. Engineers or lawyers are also acceptable. The bad daughters—well, they're the ones who run off with older boys, dye their hair brassy, barely pass high school, drop out of community college and end up working at their aunties' nail salons. Or they become writers.

These were the rules, spoken and unspoken, I'd always known. As a kid I was routinely scolded for reading too much, and I knew better than to ask to buy any books, because they were a waste of money. Writing, I learned early on, was something to do in secret.

I kept that secret for years, but finally ended up breaking it in a pretty obvious way: I wrote a memoir, called *Stealing Buddha's Dinner*, about my family leaving Vietnam in 1975, when I was eight months old, and settling in the conservative town of Grand Rapids.

When my sister read the book in manuscript form—I wanted to see what she thought of what I remembered, if our memories meshed—she said, "This could've been a whole lot worse."

"I like it," she announced, giving the book her blessing. And then: "It's funny. Vietnamese people don't do things like this. American people do."

Like most immigrants, I had learned to live a dual life—the ethnic one at home and the American one out in the world. This duality, which is central to my book, seemed to take on another layer in the actual publishing of it. Memoir *is* such an American form, not an Asian one. To tell the stories of family is to break the divide between inside and outside. My writing family stories down emphasized: I was a bad Asian daughter but an okay American one.

The memoirist can't escape having to depict other people: one's personal history always involves relationships. Which usually involve *tension* and *conflict*, words I often say when I teach, words behind so much teaching about narrative. For me, that meant writing about how silence defined my family, how we turned our attention to any other noise—radio, TV, all those generally bad '80s sounds I grew up with—instead of speaking to one another.

Silence is such an old, tedious word, seemingly unshakeable from so many Asian American experiences. It's also, inevitably, at the core of the question of why we write at all in this "truth genre." We write, of course, against the tide of silence, the same one that pushes people to say:

I'm not going to write about this until everyone else is gone.

Or: *I could never do "that" [insert: tell the truth] to my parents/family.*

Once, a student of mine declared that the whole genre of memoir was just *wrong*. He thought it was immoral, the way our writing must contain other people's histories as well as our own. Who are we, he asked, to tell these stories?

This question can be asked of fiction and poetry as well, but nonfiction has no cloak of make-believe to hide behind, no semantic scrim between narrator and author, speaker and author. Because the memoirist is the I—or at least, a version of the I—voice and perspective seem so much more fraught. Memoir cannot rest as a mere story or exploration of ideas that happen to be true. It is seen as a kind of record. And to enter into this record-keeping is to assert, audaciously, a point of view.

Mark Doty, in his essay "Return to Sender," about the writing of his memoir *Firebird*, talks about how "the mere act of describing" those we love becomes a "form of distortion"—what he calls the "betrayal built into memoir, into the telling of memories. But the alternative," he says, "is worse: are we willing to lose the past, to allow it to be erased, because it can only be partially known?" Think of all that would have been erased had Maxine Hong Kingston or Tobias Wolff or Mark Doty acquiesced to the fear of distortion.

So how about a little ruthlessness instead: write everything down first; pare away later. Because how else to find out what we are capable of discovering? And what does this genre require if not a working toward discovery? Is memoir so dangerous that the very notion of it can scare us into silence? Better, I think, to write with a little denial on our side, giving ourselves the freedom to write with clarity and honesty instead of fussy self-consciousness.

For me, denial worked so well that it wasn't until a few weeks before the publication of my book that I started really worrying. At first I didn't even recognize why I'd suddenly become a restless sleeper. But soon, panic-laced thoughts started flying through my mind, distilling into one thought that went something like, *What have I done? Who am I to tell this story?*

For good and for bad, to my family and my family's immigrant community, my book stands as a kind of document—of our story, of the Vietnamese American experience of arrival and resettlement. An ethnic American text, it seems, must always represent something else. This is a final twist to the anxiety of what we write (which applies not only to nonfiction): that our private work can become public, a living text subject to other people's interpretation and analysis.

And I did worry about my family's interpretation—that old question of *What will they think of me?* But I underestimated them. Like my sister, they were a little amused, a little baffled that anyone would want to read about our lives, but also interested in the idea that our experiences were worth writing about at all.

I'm pretty sure my father has not read my book, and I'm pretty sure he probably never will. I tell people he's not a big reader, which is true. I say he's incredibly supportive and proud, which is also true.

He shows the book to all of his friends and tries to coerce them into buying it. The book is a product to him. But he won't read it. I wonder if he doesn't want to know how I remember him or how I depict him. I don't ask, but I do ask other questions. About Vietnam, the war, how he grew up. My family talks so much when we're together now, drowning out all the background noise. They know, of course, and my father knows, too, that I'm writing it all down—and yet they keep talking.

Your Mother Should Know

SUE WILLIAM SILVERMAN

I have a secret to tell you.

Now, just so you know, I've *already* revealed, through my writing, that my father sexually molested me, that my mother didn't protect me, that my sister, to protect herself, abandoned our family as much as possible. In addition to childhood secrets, I've revealed adult secrets as well: unhappy marriages, divorces, infidelities, an eating disorder, and a sexual addiction. So you might well think that I couldn't possibly have any other secrets left to tell.

I do.

On the face of it, though, this secret I'm now going to tell may seem mild in comparison, perhaps anticlimactic.

Here it is: I received what surely must be the worst SAT scores in the history of the universe. To compound this embarrassment, I was rejected from every college to which I applied, except for a two-year division of Boston University. Even after all these years, this causes me shame.

So why tell *you*?

Or why write about things like incest and sex addiction? Isn't it difficult enough to confide our innermost secrets to a best friend or therapist, let alone complete strangers? To say nothing of risking hostility, ridicule, denial, and anger from aunts, uncles, cousins, siblings, grandparents, parents. *What will the neighbors think? What will my mother say?* Why jeopardize relationships?

Because I have to.

I write because it's a relief to hide no longer behind a veil of secrets. Growing up, I lived a double life. To the outside world, we seemed like a normal, happy family: My father had an important career first in government, then in banking. Nice houses. Nice cars. Pretty clothes. But all this seeming perfection was a veneer, a façade, for the *other* life. It masked the reality that my father sexually molested me . . . a reality never spoken aloud either in our house, in private, or in public.

As an adult, I likewise lived a double life. Even after that shaky start with those wretched SAT scores, I did graduate from college. For a while I worked on Capitol Hill. My first husband was an attorney, my second a college professor. Even divorced, I appeared like a normal, respectable adult. Yet, as with my childhood, this seeming perfection masked my messy life. For years as an adult, I was an out-of-control addict.

Now, after writing my secrets, the weight of life feels lighter. Without the burden of living a double, splintered life, I'm whole.

But what about other people involved in these secrets, especially my parents? Aren't I, in my writing, supposed to protect their privacy?

No.

I am, after all, the one who *lived* my secrets. They're mine. *I* am the owner of all the secrets that dwell in the attic of my mind. As owner, I'm free to reveal them. Since my family was involved in the creation of my secrets, I feel justified, even obliged, as a writer, to reveal the roles they played. It was *because* my father molested me that I suffered sex addiction, an eating disorder—even bad SAT scores. You see, the night before the exam, I was kept awake by him. The next morning, staring at all those questions, all those empty, blank circles waiting to be filled, I was numb. Stunned. Drowsy. Dissociated. *I* felt like a blank, empty circle.

How can I write a life, be a memoirist, without including members of my family? They are woven into the threads of every experience. If I don't write, I will once again be silenced, just like my childhood self; in essence, my father, again, will silence me. If I don't write my secrets I will, in effect, still be keeping his. Only my own words can finally fill that blank, empty space that once was me.

My main sadness as a writer and as a daughter is that I didn't write these truths while my parents were still alive. Only by telling our family truths could we have been an authentic family. Only by telling my secrets can I be an authentic woman. This is the only way for me to be an authentic writer, as well.

Writing is the way to remove the muzzle and blinders of childhood.

Why didn't I write my first memoir while my parents were still alive? I was in midtherapy when they died, not yet sure enough of my own power. For years, I remained timid, still trying to be the "good" girl my parents raised, the obedient girl who, as a child, had no choice but compliantly to let my father hurt me without saying a word. Not a whisper. Not a hint. Nothing. Even years after the abuse ended, I remained, emotionally, that wounded little girl. I didn't want to upset anyone. I didn't want to bring attention to scary secrets. I didn't want to anger my father or mother. Well into adulthood, I wanted to maintain the pretense of a perfect family. Before I began therapy, I, myself, was scared to know the truth—scared to admit to myself that my childhood was a wreck, that my "perfect" family was a lie.

What might have happened if I had written or published my books while my parents were still alive?

Perhaps they would have denied my truths, disowned me.

Would this have scared me? Yes. But would it have scared me into silence? I'd like to think the answer to that question is *No*.

Through writing, I feel my own power. Through telling my story, listening to other women's stories, I am no longer a timid little girl—even as I still, at times, get scared. But I try not to allow fear to preclude me from writing. After years of silence, I have a voice.

So how did friends and family react to my memoirs?

Well, how did *you* react when I told you I received the worst SAT scores in the history of the universe? Did you think less of me? Did you judge me? Did you assume I must be stupid? If, instead, you understood and accepted why I received these bad scores, then chances are your real friends (all the readers of your work) won't judge you, either.

But, of course, one's family is of grave concern, and family is what prohibits many people from writing and publishing their work. So let me share three stories about what happened to me when my books were published. With one book I lost someone. With the other, I gained a family. With both my books, the relationship with my sister never changed at all.

While I was married, I only hinted to my husband about the double life I led as a sex addict. After we divorced we remained friends . . . at least until *Love Sick* was published. The last pleasant phone conversation we had was right before he left for the bookstore.

Then, one day a while later, I received an angry phone call. He was angry both at the way I'd portrayed him, as well as at the fact that I hadn't been entirely honest with him during the marriage. While I couldn't fix his second concern, I think I was generous in my portrayal of him. After all, I didn't tell *his* secrets, such as—Oh, wait, memoir isn't supposed to be about revenge! Yes, I showed him as emotionally distant—which is how I described myself as well. This was our marriage. I had to be honest about it. But I was as gentle toward him (in my opinion) as possible, while still telling my secrets, still writing my story.

I don't write out of a sense of revenge. I write to understand my own story. And in *Love Sick* I was as hard, or harder, on myself, than I was on him—or anyone else. While initially I was upset about his anger, I now understand that it's his choice if he wants to be angry. I can't control his feelings. My intent wasn't to upset him. My honesty is more important to me than his anger.

But don't assume that your revelations will always result in anger or loss of relationships. You might be surprised. Here is my second story.

I began to write *Because I Remember Terror, Father, I Remember You* about two weeks after my parents died (within six days of each other), so I didn't have to worry about their reaction. I was, however, concerned about my father's large extended family, many of whom lived in Chicago, about three hours from me. But since I barely knew these cousins, uncles, and aunts—had, in fact, been isolated from them my entire life—I decided not to search them out or alert them to the book ahead of time. (I was also scared and really, *really* hoped they'd never find out!) I figured I'd let the book go out into the world and see what happened.

Initially, nothing did. In conjunction with its publication, I even authored an article in the *Chicago Tribune* about the need for child abuse to be seen as a human rights issue. Not a word. The book came out in paperback. Still nothing. Then, about three years after the initial publication . . .

It was a Friday evening about nine o'clock when the phone rang. A woman identified herself; her name sounded vaguely familiar. A second or third cousin, maybe? She told me she'd just finished reading my book.

I barely heard her next words. I sank down on the couch, gripping the phone. I thought I heard the word "sorry." Yes, she was saying she felt so sorry about what happened to me as a child. That *all* the cousins, aunts, uncles had been talking about it the last few weeks, and they were *all* sorry.

"No one knew or suspected," she said.

After this initial contact, I received e-mails, phone calls, and letters from family members I barely knew existed. Everyone was upset—but not that I had told my family secret. Rather, everyone was distressed because of what happened to me, even though my father had always been placed on a pedestal by his family. He was a true immigrant success story. He worked his way through the University of Chicago: undergraduate and law school. He held important professional positions. He made the family look good. He had a commanding, successful voice.

Now, all the members of his family heard *my* voice. Really, they heard the voice of a little girl.

I subsequently attended a large family reunion in Chicago to be officially welcomed into the fold.

The third story about my family's reaction concerns my sister. She claims she wasn't abused by our father; yet she never doubted or questioned that I was. And when I told her about the upcoming publication of my first book, she took it in stride. Did she wish, instead, I was publishing a novel? Probably. Yet she still told me she was proud. Even so, she hasn't read either of my books. At first, this upset me. Now, I understand that to read them would be too painful for her. So I simply appreciate that she's supportive. She tells her friends about the books. She buys copies of them. I feel reassured knowing that they sit in the bookcase in her home.

Grace Paley said, "Let's go forth with fear and courage to save the world."

Well, while I certainly can't claim that I myself am out to try to save the world—still, still, I do want to go forth armed with fear *and* courage to meet one other scared woman . . . and then another.

After I completed a reading at a library in Athens, Georgia, one woman waited until everyone else had departed. Approaching me, she was so scared she began to cry. She confided that I was the first person she'd told that her father had molested her. She was too traumatized even to tell a therapist.

Why did she confide in me, trust me?

Because we women now find our own home—a safe home, a home without secrets and lies—with other women. We find this new home, this community of women, by allowing our dark secrets and traumas to float free on pieces of paper out into the world. Our memoirs cast hope across the universe, hope for other women.

All I can do, as a woman and as a writer, is to write from my heart and tell my truths without worrying about the reaction of friends and family.

Why?

Women with shattered lives, women who have no voice of their own—*these* women want to read our stories. Women want to read *each other's* stories. Women want to read these stories in order to better understand their own. As Patricia Hampl says in *The Nonfictionist's Guide: On Reading and Writing Creative Nonfiction*, "You give me your story, I get mine."

I write my truths because I'm a writer. I write them because I must.

Writing about Family

HEATHER SELLERS

More than kittens, candy, or dolls, it was true: I loved houses. I memorized the parts, the possibilities: *fascia, clerestory, breezeway, ogee*. My mother always thought I would be an architect; for her, my nonverbal learning disability was not a factor. But I didn't want to build houses. I wanted to live in one. A good one. To this end, I was obsessed with floor plans. After school every day, for years, I drew floor plans for family homes. I wasn't going to become an architect, ever. I was becoming a self, drafting and organizing a personality. I was mapping a blueprint for hope.

During this time, my mother suffered from severe paranoid schizophrenia: we couldn't eat food prepared by anyone but her, and she wasn't always up for cooking. She and I lived then in a ranch house in downtown Orlando, where she was slowly, literally closing off rooms. First the Florida room was out of bounds—water problems (there were mushrooms along the baseboards). The living room wasn't safe (the doors didn't properly close, and it was true: anyone could walk in). Then my bedroom was blocked off—a wild animal had gotten in and was dramatically starving itself to death, an event we'd wait out. By winter, we were down to the kitchen, hallway, and her bedroom/bathroom. To which she required I approach on my knees—my feet were too filthy to walk on the floors.

As she closed down the rooms of our house and life became an outpost on a dark frontier, I checked out from the library *Better Homes and Gardens Building Guides*, up to the limit: five at a time. And I drew thousands of houses. Instead of playing with other children, I drew all these houses and saw the people who lived there, and watched them closely before I moved on. New house, new people. New problems.

I would have said I wasn't lonely.

I labeled each room: LR, DR, BR, BA, CL, KIT. And I kept adding rooms, expanding my facility to be inside of houses, adding breadth to my own self. Children's playroom. Study. Gallery. I read about widow's walks and porticos, and dreamed the amazing things that could happen in those places. I learned how to use dotted lines to indicate future spaces. Future bedroom. Future mother-in-law apartment. Future garage. Future swimming pool, future patio, future future.

I remember walking through the rooms, in my mind's eye, as me, Heather, an only slightly enhanced me, in beautiful dresses. I was my after-school dwelling self.

In my floor plans, something or someone wonderful was always waiting for me elsewhere in the house. A piano. A husband. An indoor fountain.

My junior year of high school required each student take a careers inventory. I was thrilled to get my results. My careers inventory indicated I was best suited for computers, nursing, forestry, or teaching, all unthinkable options. How on earth had it gotten these things? I'd put I didn't like helping people *that* much. Yes, I'd prefer to work outside, but I didn't mean in the forest. I didn't mean *work*. To counteract the gross misinterpretation of my future, in the blanks where you were to list two careers to receive more information about, I selected Electronics and Architecture.

Senior year, I took drafting class in high school. My hands sweat so much the paper dissolved, little island-shaped holes, with smeared edges. I didn't create so much as I erased. The teacher, a retired army officer, encouraged me, the only girl in the class, to drop.

I dropped. I didn't really want to draft. I wanted to live in a normal house. I wanted a family.

What I needed was a writing life.

I never considered what to write *about*; from the beginning, I wrote about my family. I write about my family in order to light the dark rooms we've lived in, and to create rooms that might hold something of the complexity of what can't be explained or understood. With all those floor plans, I *drew* myself in to this project, my life's work.

A good piece of art, like a moment with a mental patient, displays a full range of human emotion, compressed. Terror, desire, fear, guilt, joy, anger, surprise, all bundled into a single iteration. Human energy, pressed into a shape.

A floor plan, based primarily on suggestion and implication and code and fantasy, can work the same way. It's a glimpse of everything desired and known pressed into a shape and flattened out. Your couch could go here. Your happiness, here. Your breakdowns, tantrums, proposals, and drapes will all be contained in this square. Now, come down the hallway. Or, walk through walls! A floor plan, like literature, indicates shape and stabilizes hope while also giving you superpowers. You're not alone. You can turn invisible. You can always add on—this dotted line shows what comes next.

Now, as an adult I don't draw floor plans, per se, but I still spend hours and hours every day imagining myself in the context of complicated family rooms; my life is pretty much the same as it was when I was eleven years old. I go to school, teaching now instead of being taught. And I come home and I imagine families in various kinds of shapes, trying to understand what we're doing to one another inside houses. Family, for me, offers the essential map for reading the world of experience.

Finding my subject was easy; keeping it wasn't.

My first story in my first college fiction workshop was essentially a poor, fetid, short version of *Lolita*, and the teacher gently pointed this out. In class Dr. Brubaker said, "Do you know enough about a middle-aged man to write from his point of view?" The class, led by a handsome hipster named Jeff, who played guitar in a punk band, echoed the teacher in workshop, only not so gently: "It's like you just read *Lolita* or something."

I *had* just read *Lolita*. I loved that book. I thought it untoward, unseemly, unnecessary to point this out.

And in his office, later, my professor said, "What, for example, might this person, unnamed, have had for breakfast?"

I wasn't sure if I was supposed to answer or not. I wouldn't have written the story if I thought I didn't know enough about my character (who was me, just as an aged priest). Who cared what he had for breakfast? Breakfast didn't matter to this story! The story took place in the evening. On a dock. Where he/I interviewed an uncomfortable unnamed teen girl/me—what she was doing at the rectory, what they were doing on a dock, all unclear . . .

It was frustrating that no one liked the story, but their dislike wasn't an impediment, it was more a motivation. It didn't discourage me from writing more short stories—I wrote every day. In doing this work, I'd caught the wave of something unknowable and alive, and I couldn't leave it alone. It was a secret place we all have access to. *What happened here? What if I added on?* I realized, at some point, that the problem with the priest on a dock story was there was no floor plan.

The second short story I wrote went over better in my class, and so I mailed it to my mother. Not because it was about her, which it was, but because I thought it was good. Really, really good.

I didn't think she'd notice—I really didn't, though I hadn't even changed any of our names—that the story was about her and how hard it had been to have her as my mother. I believed she'd be so awed by the literary quality, she'd only focus on how thrilling it was to have given birth to a great writer.

She never mentioned the story. I never asked her if she'd received it. At some point, I realized how cruel I'd been and felt great shame.

To write about family is to plagiarize life. I believe it can be done with grace. I believe, in my case, it has been the right thing to do. But it's still stealing.

Both of my parents, who worked at real jobs sporadically and then not at all, often talked loudly and at length about the books they were going to write, as soon as they had "time." Unemployed people talking about time is confusing to a child and annoying to an adult.

Though they didn't write, my parents saw themselves as writers. I never witnessed either of my parents reading a book, ever, much less putting pen to paper, but we owned three complete sets of the collected works of Mark Twain, that ubiquitous series of dusty green volumes, spines segmented black, gold lettering quietly announcing the hilarious titles. I did not have a bed, a dresser, a bedroom, but we had enough linear feet of Mark Twain to pave a driveway.

They did not write, and I'm certain this is why I've written, in as many years, three books on the topic of writing, chapter after chapter urging writers not to delay on their projects, offering practical strategies to begin, to work cheerfully, without drama or neurosis, continue on to completion *while holding down a full-time job and being very good to your children*. The thesis and belabored point in each of these texts is: if you want to write, *please please write and don't waste time*.

My parents' fantasy writing lives gave me two things. The idea that writing literature was valuable, something to be sought, something possible. And, a free pass. If they wanted to write, somehow I felt I had permission to not only write, but to write about *them*. Somehow, if I wrote about us, I perfected us. They couldn't figure out how to write. But they could be written about and written *into*—written into my stories and poems and books.

In that first story workshop, I learned sharp lessons in what not to do (pretend I was Nabokov, pretend I was a middle-aged Catholic priest, pretend capital letters were politically troublesome for me personally, use onionskin).

I was crucified in workshop; I didn't mind, in fact, I could take it. The embarrassment felt familiar. I was raised by violent, unpredictable, troubled people. I could survive this mild-by-comparison public immolation. In fact, brutal workshop was easier than parties, friendship, the mall. In the normal world, I was lost and anxious. In workshop, that circle of pecking and envy and criticism and close looking, I thrived. And I found a subject that pleased my peers and professors. My family.

I just started writing down everything that had happened. Instead of Bs, now I got As. Punk rock Jeff asked me out. I published.

One day I went to my mailbox and found a rumpled brown mailer. Inside was a manuscript and a tiny slip of thin paper, paper clipped to the story. It was my mother's perfect script. The note read, "I know you are very, very busy, but perhaps you might have time to critique!" She also said she was happy to be writing again and she'd drawn a cheery little pig, with a perky snout and a smile. He was holding a balloon.

The story, typed on onionskin, was titled, "The Daughter's Visit."

I read the story greedily, standing in the driveway, my sweaty fingers sticking in a pleasing way to the pages, my mother's pages. She'd written the story of my coming home with my boyfriend to see her. In her story, the daughter was selfish and demanding. The mother tried to please this girl, but there were limits. The kindly mother had her own life: her husband, her garden, and her dreams, things the daughter didn't even notice at all.

I begged her to write more stories. "Send them to me!" I said. I can't remember, but I am sure I had suggestions, workshop suggestions, perhaps more subtext in the dialogue, or could we see the daughter? What she was wearing? What did she like to eat for breakfast?

I give my students four pieces of advice—it takes all semester.

1. Don't show your work to your family or your lover, ever. Do not do this work in order to be seen, to be right. Do it in order to see. Look at it—just you and work—longer, alone. Keep your work secret, and it takes on a life of its own. Pretend no one you know will ever read it and the rest of the world needs your truth.

2. Use up your secrets. Things are worse than you thought and more beautiful and interesting than you thought.

3. Write about the people for whom you have felt all the colors of the emotions, red fire, blue sadness, black rage, green tolerance, sunny love. Start with the family, find out something about yourself, and then leave town, move on. Or not. Start out by writing those shapes you know so well, what you can draw with your eyes closed.

4. Don't start writing until you've drawn the floor plan for your story. Where are the closets? Where is the door? Literally.

Gratitude

To all the contributors, who so generously shared their stories.

To Kristen Elias Rowley, humanities editor at the University of Nebraska Press, who believed in the good this collection could do.

To Monica Rentfrow and Sindu Sathiyaseelan, editorial assistants, for their engaged reading, thoughtful suggestions, and scrupulous care, and to the University of Nebraska–Lincoln for providing assistant support for this project.

To my agent Mitchell Waters, for his ongoing help and his faith in my work.

To my family: source of stories, source of trouble, source of love. Source.

Source Acknowledgments

Contributors

FAITH ADIELE is author of *Meeting Faith*, which won the PEN Beyond Margins Award for Memoir, and writer/subject/narrator of *My Journey Home*, a PBS documentary about her Nigerian/Nordic/American family. Her essays and memoirs have appeared in *O Magazine*, *Ploughshares*, *Transition*, *Ms.*, *Essence*, *Fourth Genre*, *Creative Nonfiction*, and numerous anthologies. She has taught workshops on memoir in Accra, Bali, Chautauqua, Geneva, Iowa, Johannesburg, San Francisco, and Whidbey Island. Adiele currently serves as Distinguished Visiting Writer at Mills College in Oakland, California, where she is finishing a family memoir that will complete the story begun in the film.

PAUL AUSTIN is working on his second memoir with the working title *Beautiful Eyes: Down Syndrome, Fatherhood, and What It Means to Be Human*, which is forthcoming from W. W. Norton. His first book, *Something for the Pain: One Doctor's Account of Life and Death in the ER*, was given a starred review by *Library Journal*. The *Boston Globe* called it "a stunning account of the chaos of the emergency room." Father of three. Married for twenty-seven years and it seems like a day. Rides a bike to work. Schwinn. Pedal brakes. Whitewall tires.

ALISON BECHDEL drew the self-syndicated comic strip *Dykes to Watch Out For* for many years. Her 2006 graphic memoir *Fun Home: A Family Tragicomic* was a finalist for the National Book Critics Circle Award and, in an exciting moment for graphic narrative, was named Book of the Year by *Time* magazine. She retired her comic strip in 2008 to write and draw a second memoir, *Are You My Mother: A Comic Drama*.

RUTH BEHAR was born in Havana, Cuba, and grew up in New York City. She is a professor of anthropology at the University of Michigan and has received the honor of a MacArthur Fellows Award. She is acclaimed for her ethnographic writing about Spain, Mexico, and Cuba, and also writes personal essays, poetry, and fiction. Her latest book, *An Island Called Home: Returning to Jewish Cuba*, is an ethnographic memoir about searching for lost places.

JOY CASTRO is the author of *The Truth Book: A Memoir*, which was selected as a BookSense Notable Book by the American Booksellers Association, the literary thriller *Hell or High Water*, and the essay collection *Island of Bones*. Her work has appeared in *Fourth Genre*, *Seneca Review*, *Indiana Review*, *Texas Review*, *North American Review*, and the *New York Times Magazine*. She teaches at the University of Nebraska–Lincoln.

JILL CHRISTMAN's memoir, *Darkroom: A Family Exposure*, won the AWP Award Series in Creative Nonfiction and was reissued in paperback in fall 2011. Her recent essays have been published in *Barrelhouse*, *Brevity*, *Descant*, *Literary Mama*, *Mississippi Review*, *River Teeth*, and many other magazines and anthologies. She teaches creative nonfiction in Ashland University's low-residency MFA program and at Ball State University in Muncie, where she lives with her husband, writer Mark Neely, and their two children.

JUDITH ORTIZ COFER is the author of books in various genres, including *Silent Dancing: A Partial Remembrance of a Puerto Rican Childhood* and *The Latin Deli*. She is the recipient of a Pushcart Prize, the O. Henry Prize, the Anisfield-Wolf Book Award, and the Reforma Pura Belpré Medal. Her most recent books are for children. They include *A bailar: Let's Dance*, a bilingual picture book, and *Animal Jamboree: Latino Folktales*, a bilingual reader for older children. Another picture book, *The Poet Upstairs*, is forthcoming. She teaches creative writing at the University of Georgia.

RIGOBERTO GONZÁLEZ is the author of eight books, including the memoir *Butterfly Boy: Memories of a Chicano Mariposa*. The recipient of a Guggenheim, an NEA, the American Book Award, and a New York Foundation for the Arts fellowship, he writes a Latino book column for the *El Paso Times* of Texas. He is contributing editor for *Poets & Writers Magazine*, on the board of directors of the National Book Critics Circle, and on the advisory circle of Con Tinta, a collective of Chicano/Latino activist writers. He lives in New York City and is associate professor of English at Rutgers-Newark, the State University of New Jersey.

ARIEL GORE is the founding editor of *Hip Mama* and the author of seven books, including the memoir *Atlas of the Human Heart*, *The Traveling Death and Resurrection Show*, and *Bluebird: Women and the New Psychology of Happiness*.

STEPHANIE ELIZONDO GRIEST has mingled with the Russian mafia, polished Chinese propaganda, and belly danced with Cuban rumba queens. These adventures inspired her award-winning memoirs *Around the Bloc: My Life in Moscow, Beijing, and Havana* and *Mexican Enough: My Life between the Borderlines*, as well as the guidebook *100 Places Every Woman Should Go*. As a national correspondent for *The Odyssey*, she once drove forty-five thousand miles across America in a Honda hatchback named Bertha. She has won a Hodder fellowship to Princeton, a Richard Margolis Award for Social Justice Reporting, and a Lowell Thomas Travel Journalism Gold Prize.

ALLISON HEDGE COKE's memoir *Rock, Ghost, Willow, Deer*, which chronicled her early life as the second daughter of the village crazy, was an AIROS Book-of-the-Month. Other books include *Dog Road Woman*, which won the American Book Award, as well as *Off-Season City Pipe* and the verse play *Blood Run*, both of which won Wordcraft's Writer of the Year. Fiction publications include short stories in *American Fiction* and *Black Renaissance Noire*. Hedge Coke has edited eight additional collections, including *Sing* and *Effigies*. She came of age cropping tobacco, working fields and waters, and working in factories.

ROBIN HEMLEY is the author of ten books of nonfiction and fiction, including the memoirs *Nola: A Memoir of Faith, Art, and Madness* and *Do Over*. He is also the author of the popular craft books *Turning Life into Fiction* and *A Field Guide for Immersion Writing: Memoir, Journalism, and Travel*. His book of short stories, *Reply All*, was published by Break Away Books, an imprint of Indiana University Press. He is the director of the nonfiction writing program at the University of Iowa and founder of the NonfictioNow Conference.

RICHARD HOFFMAN is author of *Half the House: a Memoir*; three poetry collections, *Without Paradise*, *Emblem*, and *Gold Star Road*, winner of the 2006 Barrow Street Press Poetry Prize and the New England Poetry Club's Sheila Motton Book Award; as well as the short story collection *Interference & Other Stories*. He teaches at Emerson College, and currently serves as chair of PEN New England.

SUSAN ITO is a creative nonfiction coeditor and former columnist at *Literary Mama*. She is the coeditor of the anthology *A Ghost at Heart's Edge: Stories and Poems of Adoption*. Her work has appeared in *Growing Up Asian American*, *Making More Waves*, CHOICE, *Hip Mama*, the *Bellevue Literary Review*, and elsewhere. She has been awarded fellowships at the MacDowell Colony, Blue Mountain Center, and Hedgebrook.

AARON RAZ LINK is a writer, performer, and teacher. *What Becomes You*, his memoir in two voices with his mother, Hilda Raz, was a 2008 Lambda Literary Award finalist in both Men's Memoir and Transgender Writing. His work can be found in *Brevity, Parabola, Prairie Schooner, Water~Stone Review*, and *Fourth Genre*. He is currently finishing a book about performing, and he lives and teaches in Portland, Oregon.

PAUL LISICKY is the author of the memoir *Famous Builder*, the novels *Lawnboy* and *The Burning House*, and the collection *Unbuilt Projects*. His stories and essays have appeared in *Fence, Iowa Review, Ploughshares, The Rumpus, Story Quarterly*, and *Tin House*, and have been widely anthologized. He has taught in the writing programs at Cornell University, New York University, Rutgers-Newark, Sarah Lawrence, and the University of North Carolina Wilmington. He's currently the New Voices Professor in the MFA program at Rutgers-Camden. A new memoir, *The Narrow Door*, is forthcoming in 2014.

LORRAINE M. LÓPEZ's first book of fiction, *Soy la Avon Lady*, won the inaugural Miguel Marmól Prize. Her YA novel *Call Me Henri* was awarded the Paterson Prize, and her novel *The Gifted Gabaldón Sisters* was a 2008 Borders/Las Comadres Selection. López's short story collection *Homicide Survivors Picnic* was a finalist for the 2010 PEN/Faulkner Prize. She edited a collection of essays titled *An Angle of Vision*. Her novel *The Realm of Hungry Spirits* was released in 2011. Recently she has coedited, with Blas Falconer, a memoir collection titled *The Other Latin@*.

KAREN SALYER MCELMURRAY is author of the memoir *Surrendered Child: A Birth Mother's Journey*, recipient of the AWP Award for Creative Nonfiction; and of *Strange Birds in the Tree of Heaven*, winner of the Chaffin Award for Appalachian Writing. Her newest novel, *The Motel of the Stars*, has been nominated for the Weatherford Prize in Fiction, was a Lit Life Novel of the Year, and was named Editor's Pick by Oxford American. Associate professor in creative writing at Georgia College and State University, McElmurray is creative nonfiction editor for *Arts and Letters: A Journal of Contemporary Culture*.

DINTY W. MOORE is author of *Crafting the Personal Essay: A Guide for Writing and Publishing Creative Nonfiction*, as well as the memoir *Between Panic and Desire*, winner of the Grub Street Nonfiction Book Prize in 2009. Moore has published essays and stories in *Southern Review, Georgia Review, Harpers*, the *New York Times Sunday Magazine*, the *Philadelphia Inquirer Magazine, Gettysburg Review, Utne Reader*, and *Crazyhorse*, among numerous other venues. He is a professor of nonfiction writing at Ohio University.

BICH MINH NGUYEN's memoir *Stealing Buddha's Dinner* received the PEN/ Jerard Award from the PEN American Center and was named a Chicago Tribune Best Book of the Year and a Kiriyama Prize Notable Book. Her novel *Short Girls* received an American Book Award in Fiction.

SUSAN OLDING is the author of *Pathologies: A Life in Essays*, winner of the Creative Nonfiction Collective's Readers' Choice Award for 2008. Her poetry and prose have appeared widely in literary journals, magazines, and anthologies across Canada and the United States. She has been a finalist for a National Magazine Award, two Western Magazine Awards, and a CBC Literary Award; and she is the recipient of a number of prizes and honors, including the Brenda Ueland Prose Prize for Literary Nonfiction. Born in Toronto, she currently lives with her family in Kingston, Ontario.

RALPH JAMES SAVARESE teaches at Grinnell College. *Newsweek* called his recent book *Reasonable People: A Memoir of Autism and Adoption* a "real life love story and an urgent manifesto for the rights of people with neurological disabilities." His poems, translations, essays, criticism, and opinion pieces have appeared, among other places, in *American Poetry Review*, *Sewanee Review*, *Southwest Review*, *New England Review*, *Fourth Genre*, *Modern Poetry in Translation*, *Leviathan*, *Disability Studies Quarterly*, the *New York Times*, and the *LA Times*.

MIMI SCHWARTZ is the author of five books, most recently *Good Neighbors, Bad Times: Echoes of My Father's German Village*, winner of a ForeWord Award for Best Memoir in 2008. Other books include *Thoughts from a Queen-Sized Bed* and *Writing True: The Art and Craft of Creative Nonfiction*. Her short work has appeared in *AGNI*, *Missouri Review*, *Fourth Genre*, *Creative Nonfiction*, *Arts & Letters*, and *Writer's Chronicle*, among others—with seven being Notables in *Best American Essays*. She is professor emerita of Richard Stockton College and lives in Princeton, New Jersey.

SANDRA SCOFIELD is the author of seven novels and a memoir, *Occasions of Sin*. A National Book Award finalist, she won the Texas Institute of Letters Best Fiction Award in 1997 and was a 1991 National Endowment for the Arts Fellow. She teaches at the Iowa Summer Writing Festival and in the low-residency MFA program at Pine Manor College in Boston. Her craft book for writers is titled *The Scene: A Primer for the Fiction Writer*. She is presently at work on a book about her grandmother. She divides her time between Portland, Oregon, and Missoula, Montana.

HEATHER SELLERS is author of the memoir *You Don't Look Like Anyone I Know*, an Oprah Book of the Month Club selection and a *New York Times* Editor's Choice, and the winner of a Michigan Notable Book Award and a Friends of American Writers Award. She is also the author of *Georgia Under Water*, a children's book, three poetry collections, and two memoir-handbooks on the writing life, *Page after Page* and *Chapter after Chapter*. Her textbook for introductory creative writing students, *The Practice of Creative Writing*, is out in a new edition from Bedford St. Martin's. She is a professor of English at Hope College.

SUE WILLIAM SILVERMAN's memoir *Love Sick: One Woman's Journey through Sexual Addiction* is also a Lifetime television movie. Her first memoir, *Because I Remember Terror, Father, I Remember You*, won the AWP Award in Creative Nonfiction, while her craft book *Fearless Confessions: A Writer's Guide to Memoir* was awarded Honorable Mention in *ForeWord Review*'s Book-of-the-Year Award in the category of Writing. Three of her essays won contests with *Hotel Amerika*, *Mid-American Review*, and *Water~Stone Review*. She teaches in the MFA program at Vermont College of Fine Arts.

CPSIA information can be obtained
at www.ICGtesting.com
Printed in the USA
LVHW111513080320
649328LV00003BA/578